The Berkshire Studies in European History

GENERAL EDITORS

RICHARD A. NEWHALL
LAURENCE B. PACKARD
SIDNEY R. PACKARD

Berkshire Studies in European History

Under the Editorship of

Richard A. Newhall, Laurence B. Packard and Sidney R. Packard

THE CRUSADES
RICHARD A. NEWHALL, *Williams College*

EUROPE AND THE CHURCH UNDER INNOCENT III
SIDNEY R. PACKARD, *Smith College*

THE COMMERCIAL REVOLUTION
LAURENCE B. PACKARD, *Amherst College*

THE INDUSTRIAL REVOLUTION
FREDERICK C. DIETZ, *University of Illinois*

GEOGRAPHICAL BASIS OF EUROPEAN HISTORY
J. K. WRIGHT, *American Geographical Society*

THE ENLIGHTENED DESPOTS
GEOFFREY BRUUN, *New York University*

ORGANIZATION OF MEDIEVAL CHRISTIANITY
SUMMERFIELD BALDWIN, *Western Reserve University*

THE AGE OF LOUIS XIV
LAURENCE B. PACKARD, *Amherst College*

THE SECOND HUNDRED YEARS WAR, 1689-1815
ARTHUR H. BUFFINTON, *Williams College*

IMPERIALISM AND NATIONALISM IN THE FAR EAST
DAVID E. OWEN, *Yale University*

EUROPEAN IMPERIALISM IN AFRICA
HALFORD L. HOSKINS, *Tufts College*

THE BRITISH EMPIRE-COMMONWEALTH
REGINALD G. TROTTER, *Queen's University*

MEDIEVAL SLAVDOM AND THE RISE OF RUSSIA
FRANK NOWAK, *Boston University*

IMPERIAL SPAIN
EDWARD DWIGHT SALMON, *Amherst College*

THE CHURCH IN THE ROMAN EMPIRE
ERWIN R. GOODENOUGH, *Yale University*

NATIONALISM IN THE BALKANS, 1800-1930
W. M. GEWEHR, *American University*

IMPERIAL RUSSIA, 1801-1917
M. KARPOVICH, *Harvard University*

THE RUSSIAN REVOLUTION, 1917-1931
GEORGE VERNADSKY, *Yale University*

THE FRENCH REVOLUTION, 1789-1799
LEO GERSHOY, *Long Island University*

THE AGE OF METTERNICH, 1814-1848
ARTHUR MAY, *University of Rochester*

A HISTORY OF GEOGRAPHICAL DISCOVERY, 1400-1800
JAMES E. GILLESPIE, *Pennsylvania State College*

CALVINISM AND THE RELIGIOUS WARS
FRANKLIN C. PALM, *University of California*

TRIPLE ALLIANCE AND TRIPLE ENTENTE
BERNADOTTE E. SCHMITT, *University of Chicago*

BUSINESS IN THE MIDDLE AGES
SUMMERFIELD BALDWIN, *Western Reserve University*

THE RISE OF BRANDENBURG-PRUSSIA TO 1786
SIDNEY B. FAY, *Harvard University*

GERMANY SINCE 1918
FREDERICK L. SCHUMAN, *Williams College*

THE SECOND HUNDRED YEARS WAR
1689-1815

BY

ARTHUR H. BUFFINTON

ASSISTANT PROFESSOR OF HISTORY
WILLIAMS COLLEGE

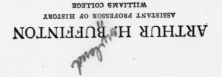

NEW YORK

HENRY HOLT AND COMPANY

11542 57

October, 1939

D
286
.B8

PREFACE

The college teacher of general European history is always confronted with the task of finding adequate reading for his classes which is neither too specialized and technical nor too elementary. For many topics, including several of the greatest importance, no such material is at the moment available. Moreover, in too many instances, good reading which undeniably does exist is in the form of a chapter in a larger work and is therefore too expensive for adoption as required reading under normal conditions.

The Berkshire Studies in European History have been planned to meet this situation. The topics selected for treatment are those on which there is no easily accessible reading of appropriate length adequate for the needs of a course in general European history. The authors, all experienced teachers, are in nearly every instance actively engaged in the class room and intimately acquainted with its problems. They will avoid a merely elementary presentation of facts, giving instead an interpretive discussion suited to the more mature point of view of college students.

No pretense is made, of course, that these *Studies* are contributions to historical literature in the scholarly sense. Each author, nevertheless, is sufficiently a specialist in the period of which he writes to be familiar with the sources and to have used the latest scholarly contributions to his subject. In order that those who desire to read further on any topic may have some guid-

v

ance short bibliographies of works in western European languages are given, with particular attention to books of recent date.

Each Study is designed as a week's reading. The division into three approximately equal chapters, many of them self-contained and each suitable for one day's assignment, should make the series as a whole easily adaptable to the present needs of college classes. The editors have attempted at every point to maintain and emphasize this fundamental flexibility.

Maps and diagrams will occasionally be furnished with the text when specially needed but a good historical atlas, such as that of Shepherd, is presupposed throughout.

R. A. N.
I. B. P.
S. R. P.

CONTENTS

THE SECOND
HUNDRED YEARS WAR
1689–1815

CHAPTER I

THE BALANCE OF POWER

Between 1689 and 1815 England and France fought seven separate wars, known collectively as the Second Hundred Years' War. No one of the wars was a duel between these two states, but in each of them one or more of the other European powers were engaged. Moreover, as each had possessions and interests in many parts of the world, the conflict was not confined to the continent of Europe. Wherever the two powers and their allies were in contact, in North America and the West Indies, on the west coast of Africa, in India and its surrounding waters, there also Englishmen and Frenchmen and their native allies engaged in combat. In certain of its phases, indeed, this may be called the first World War.

For so extensive and prolonged a conflict the causes cannot have been slight or transient. They were, in fact, interwoven with the whole fabric of the state policy of the time. The wars were but the more violent aspects of a rivalry which in one form or other existed throughout the whole period,—a rivalry which was not appeased until certain issues were definitely settled. Broadly speaking there were two principal sets of causes for this rivalry, one having to do with the relations of England to the continent and the maintenance of the balance of power, the other with questions of commercial and colonial competition. In each of the separate contests now one set of causes predominated, now the other, but in each both were present to a greater or less degree.

3

In the two centuries and a quarter which had elapsed since the close of the First Hundred Years' War England and France had been reorganized in something like their modern form, and each had developed a characteristic set of policies and interests. France had sought leadership among the continental states and had just triumphed in a prolonged contest with the House of Hapsburg. England, practically excluded from continental affairs by her defeat in the First Hundred Years' War, had sought wealth and power in the development of commerce and a colonial empire. It was only when France began to rival England as a commercial and colonial power, and when the predominance of France on the continent appeared to threaten the commercial interests and the security of England, that a clash of interest developed between them.

The immediate causes of the war may be traced to the period marked in England by the restoration of the Stuarts in the person of Charles II (1660), in France by the assumption of complete control of affairs by the young king Louis XIV (1661). It was at this time that France, already enjoying a position of ascendency among the continental powers, set out, under the leadership of Colbert, to challenge England and Holland in the race for commercial and colonial empire. The statesmen of that period were all believers in the efficacy of the mercantile system, and it was to the policies of that system that Colbert turned naturally in his efforts to make France a great commercial and colonial power. Mercantilism has been aptly described as "a system of statecraft rather than of economics." Its primary purpose was to increase the national power by increasing the national wealth, and its immediate object was to make the state as far as possible self-sufficing, for economic independence was considered to be almost as necessary as political independence. Hence the whole system of protective tariffs, navigation laws, state-chartered commercial companies, bounties, and government subsidies so familiar to all students of Mercantilism.

In applying these principles to stimulate the trade and industry of France Colbert inevitably aroused the opposition of France's rivals. With the Dutch a tariff war resulted, soon followed by a French attack upon Holland which for a time threatened the very existence of the Dutch Republic. It was during this conflict, largely commercial in origin, that there rose to power in Holland the third William of Orange, who later, as William III of England, was to prove the nemesis of Louis XIV.

In England the cries of English manufacturers who found French goods competing successfully with their own in the home market were soon heard in Parliament. English merchants also complained of French competition in the East and West Indies, in Africa, and in the Baltic. Statesmen and economists were alarmed at the unfavorable balance of trade, for it was estimated that England imported annually from France goods to the value of a million pounds more than the total of her exports to France. The cry arose for a commercial treaty, for a higher tariff, for an absolute prohibition of trade. The attack of France upon Holland increased the alarm, and in 1678 Parliament passed an act prohibiting trade with France for three years. From this time until the commercial treaty of 1786 was signed trade with France was either prohibited or burdened with such heavy duties that legitimate commerce between the two nations was almost impossible.

Colbert's mercantilist policy was also responsible for the beginning of acute Anglo-French colonial rivalry. Mercantilist statesmen regarded colonies as a highly desirable, almost necessary, adjunct to the national economy. They were to serve as sources of supply for raw materials and tropical foodstuffs, and as markets for the surplus of national manufactures. Trade between them and the mother country would also stimulate the development of the national merchant marine, which in that day had a very definite connection with naval power. In 1660 France had only feeble settlements in Canada and the West Indies, as yet of little economic value. To increase the number of existing settlements, to develop the resources of those already in existence, and to secure for France a share of the trade of Africa and India became the care of Colbert. All this constituted another challenge to France's commercial rivals.

French interest in the colonies at this time was also greatly stimulated by the missionary labors of the Jesuits among the Indians of North America. Their sufferings and heroic endeavors aroused an interest in quarters where the commercial value of colonies was little appreciated, among the courtiers and in the king himself, with whom the Jesuits were in high favor. Thus the pious of both sexes among the higher classes were induced to use their influence and their wealth to promote the extension of French power in the New World.

Hitherto there had been no serious conflict between the French and English in America. Both had settlements among the lesser islands of the West Indies, but there were still many unoccupied islands. On the North American continent the feeble French settlements in Canada and Acadia were separated from the

more populous English colonies along the Atlantic seaboard by many leagues of ocean and trackless forest.
The rivalry which developed at this time between them
was much more a commercial than a territorial rivalry.
Only dimly did the French perceive that the future of
the continent was at stake; the English as yet perceived
it not at all. Furthermore, in its earliest phases this
rivalry was one which concerned the two governments
and their clashing policies in America far more than
the settlers themselves.

There were two principal areas of conflict, the seaboard area of Newfoundland, Acadia and New England, and the inland region where French Canada
clashed with the English Hudson's Bay posts on the
one side and with the colony of New York on the other.

In the first of these areas the principal question in
dispute was the control of the fisheries of the Acadian
and Newfoundland banks, richer, as one French writer
said, than the mines of Peru. Newfoundland was fre-
quented largely by fishermen from Europe, but both
French and English had settlements upon the island.
The Acadian fisheries, on the other hand, were exploited largely by the fishermen of New England, who
not only monopolized the fisheries but traded with the
scattered French population of that country. The
Acadian French were farmers and fur-traders and
cared little about the fisheries. Not so the French government, which, beginning about 1682, made a determined effort to break up the trade between New England and Acadia and to exclude the New England
fishermen from Acadian waters.

In the second area of conflict it was a question of
the fur trade. Albany was the most important
center of this trade in English North America. The
fur trade was also the chief staple of Canada, the basis

of its economic existence. Both Albany and Montreal, the center of the Canadian fur trade, drew the bulk of their furs from the same region, the vast territory stretching from the Great Lakes to Hudson's Bay, but more especially from the peninsula between lakes Ontario and Huron, the present province of Ontario. In this economic conflict the English had the advantage of cheaper goods. They were also not hampered by any scruples concerning the effects of liquor upon the Indians, as were the French, for the Jesuits regarded the sale of liquor as an obstacle to the success of their missionary labors. The French were already feeling the competition of Albany when the establishment by the English government of the Hudson's Bay Company (1670) threatened them in another quarter.

Whereas the fisheries were exploited directly by the white men, the fur trade depended upon the Indians. Hence the question of the fur trade was complicated by questions of Indian politics. The French, on their arrival in Canada, had cultivated the friendship of the Algonquin tribes inhabiting that country. Later they had also gained the friendship of the tribes about the Great Lakes. In so doing they incurred the enmity of the powerful Iroquois confederacy, resident in the Mohawk valley and westward, which had a standing feud with the Indian nations on all sides of them. Procuring arms from the Dutch at Fort Orange (Albany), and, after the English conquest of New Netherland (1664), from their English successors, the Iroquois preyed upon the French settlements and carried destruction far and wide among the Indian allies of the French.

The danger which threatened Canada was a double one. For more than fifty years after its establishment the very existence of the colony was threatened.

It was not, in fact, until the efforts of Colbert and Louis XIV bore fruit that the colony was safe from destruction. But a scarcely less serious peril remained. If the French could not protect their Indian allies from the Iroquois, the latter would destroy or subjugate them, and the fur trade of the interior would be directed through the Mohawk valley to Albany. Canada would then be faced with economic stagnation, perhaps with ruin.

In this contest the English at first played but a passive part, selling the Iroquois arms and profiting from their successes. The French, however, suspected them of egging on the Iroquois. They also saw that it would be almost impossible to bring the Iroquois to terms so long as they could count upon English support. The French, therefore, tried all means to meet the danger. They sent Jesuits among the Iroquois, only to reap a fresh crop of martyrs. French officials advised the conquest or purchase of New York, but the King of England was not disposed to sell, nor the French government at this time to provoke a war. Finally, the French conceived the idea of establishing their hold over the nations of the interior by the erection at strategic points of forts, which would also serve as trading posts and mission stations. Thus the West would become a French preserve, the Iroquois would be curbed, and the English confined to the Atlantic seaboard.

The English were slow to awaken to the implications of this policy, but in the decade preceding the first Anglo-French war Governor Thomas Dongan of New York prepared to checkmate the French by taking the Iroquois under his protection and by sending trading parties from Albany to the West. Thus at the moment when war broke out in Europe (1689) the relations of New York and Canada were strained to the breaking point. It was a clash of rival imperialisms.

In the Acadian area, also, Indian relationships played a part. Here the rapidly expanding English population came into conflict with the Abnaki tribes of the Kennebec and Penobscot region, who began to look to the French for support and assistance. Here also there was a territorial dispute, the English claiming as far north as the river St. Croix, the French as far south as the Kennebec. Realizing that it was to their interest to prevent the English from occupying the disputed area, the French assumed the rôle of protectors of the Abnaki, and a new threat to the friendly relations of New England and the French appeared.

In this way there developed in America, in the decade preceding 1689, a rough balance of power. On the one hand were the French of Acadia and Canada allied to the Abnaki and the Lake tribes, on the other the English of New York and New England allied to the Iroquois. When James II mounted the throne in succession to his brother everything pointed to an Anglo-French colonial war; during his reign matters grew worse rather than better. The French raided the posts of the Hudson's Bay Company, captured New England fishing vessels on the coast of Acadia, despatched punitive expeditions against the Iroquois, and captured the English trading parties which Dongan sent to the West. In 1688 an Indian war broke out in Maine, which the English attributed to French instigation. The English retaliated by breaking up the attempts of the French to establish an Acadian fishery and by threatening to back up the Iroquois by force of arms; the latter, assured of English support, continued their raids upon the Indian allies of the French.

As yet, however, it suited the policy of the home

governments to keep the peace in America. Kings and ministers were primarily interested in the affairs of Europe, and were not yet disposed to regard colonial rivalries as in themselves a sufficient cause for war. Thus the diplomats of the two powers were still seeking a formula for reconciling conflicting colonial interests, when events in England revolutionized the relations of the two governments and precipitated a general conflict.

The immediate cause of the outbreak of the Second Hundred Years' War is to be found not in commercial or colonial rivalry, but in the general state of European politics at this time, and the relation thereto of the English domestic situation. The outstanding development in international affairs in the second half of the seventeenth century was the rise of France to a position of unquestioned predominance. Of the greater continental powers Spain was sunk in decay, Austria was weakened by internal stresses and by conflict with the Turks. Holland counted as a great power because of its wealth and its navy, but it was not a great military power. England, which under Cromwell had risen to a place of unparalleled influence, under the later Stuarts tended to become a satellite of France.

The reason for this astonishing change in the position of England is to be found in the policy of the later Stuart kings. Once restored to the throne, Charles II sought to regain some measure of the royal power. The son of a French Catholic mother, he sought to reestablish Catholicism in England. Both these policies ran counter to the wishes of the great majority of his subjects, and soon Parliament began to manifest its displeasure by withholding supplies. The only way Charles could nullify this opposition, short of attempting a political revolution, was to become the pensioner of the French king. In this way he gained a measure of independence of Parliament, but at the price of a subservience to France which greatly furthered the ambitions of Louis XIV.

The steady growth of French power and the apparent insatiability of Louis' ambitions soon awakened alarm among English statesmen for the balance of power. For England the question of the balance of power has always been mainly a question of security. Inferior at that time in population and in military organization to the larger continental states, England owed its security to its insular position and to its navy. If one continental power were to become much stronger than the others, and if, in addition, that power possessed also considerable naval strength, the security of England would be menaced. Furthermore, if this great power occupied such a position as to threaten England directly, the situation would appear still more alarming. By its very position, just across the English Channel, France was so situated as to make England exceedingly sensitive to any marked increase of French power in Europe.

England has also been extremely sensitive to the fate of the Low Countries, including both Holland and Belgium, and this also for reasons of national security. The Channel ports of France are not suitable for naval bases, but in Belgium and Holland are several admirable harbors. "It may almost be said," writes a modern English naval expert, "that the dominant note of English foreign policy from time immemorial has been to prevent either France or Spain securing naval stations beyond the Straits of Dover." The early wars of Louis XIV aroused alarm concerning French ambitions in this region. In his first war Louis gained much of Flanders, in his second he threatened to overthrow the Dutch Republic. The effect upon English opinion was almost magical. Having hitherto regarded the Dutch as their chief commercial rivals, the English at first acquiesced in the alliance which Charles in 1670 concluded with Louis against them, but very shortly after the war began public opinion forced Charles to make peace with the Dutch, and it was on the point of compelling him to fight France when Louis, recognizing the shift in English opinion, made peace himself.

This was to a certain extent a positive advantage to Charles, because it afforded Louis visible proof of the strength of anti-French feeling in England, and thus made it easier for Charles to extract subsidies from the French king. But the more independent Charles became of Parliament, the more unpopular did his connection with France become, and to the great majority of Englishmen France began to appear as the enemy of their political liberties and of their parliamentary system of government.

Even more disturbing to Anglo-French friendship was the question of religion. If there was one thing upon which the vast majority of Englishmen were united, it was in their hostility to the Church of Rome. This Charles had the good sense to realize, and therefore he had abandoned his plan of restoring Catholicism in England. Not so his brother and successor James, who, more blind to public opinion and more zealously Catholic than Charles, exerted all his influence to promote the cause of Catholicism. In this he counted upon the support of Louis XIV, who had just alarmed the Protestant world by revoking the Edict of Nantes. To all Protestants,—and they constituted nine-tenths of the people of England,—it was plain that the security of Protestantism required that the connection between the Stuart house and France should be broken.

For eventual deliverance from these dangers to their civil and religious liberty the people of England began to look to William of Orange, Stadtholder of the Netherlands. William was both the cousin and the son-in-law of James, and his wife Mary stood next in line of succession to the English throne. The majority of Englishmen were content to wait for the time of their deliverance until James should die, but when in 1688 James's second wife bore him a son, all parties joined in the invitation to William to come and deliver them.

Here was the opportunity for which William had long been waiting. As ruler of Holland he wished to make his country secure against French attack; as a European statesman he wished to curb the ambitions of Louis XIV and to restore the balance of power. Already he had made a defensive alliance with Sweden and Brandenburg. He knew also that to check the power of Louis XIV the Emperor had formed the League of Augsburg, including Austria, Spain, and most of the German states. Recalling, however, that during the Dutch war a combination of the principal continental powers had been none too successful against the French king, William argued that the aid of England was necessary to the success of any coalition against France. He therefore prepared to accept the English invitation.

William's preparations were soon discovered by Louis, and it lay within his power, by attacking Holland, to keep William from making the attempt. Believing, however, that an invasion of England by William would be the beginning of a long civil war in that island, Louis despatched his armies into Germany, hoping to force the Emperor and the German princes to come to terms. In both calculations Louis was mistaken. The Emperor did not come to terms; in England there was no long struggle. The power of James II crumbled at a blow, and within a few weeks from the time William landed, James was a fugitive at the French court. In a few weeks more William and Mary had accepted the English crown from the hands of Parliament, and war had been declared against France.

The issues of the war which thus began were far from simple. Louis had not willed the war, and for him it was defensive from the start. For William it was a war for the security of Holland and for the restoration of the balance of power. For the English people it was a war to protect the national religion and constitutional government against a Catholic king who was trying to subvert both with the assistance of France. Although French attacks upon the English in America were cited by William as one of the reasons for the English declaration of war, the colonial conflict was for both French and English a side issue, and so it remained until the questions raised by the English and European situation were settled.

In a very real sense this was King William's War. His was the task of keeping the English throne, of securing the co-operation of people to whom he was a foreigner in a war the larger objects of which they did not grasp, of building up a coalition sufficiently strong to outweigh the power of France, of so directing the course of the war as to bring France to terms. He had to be diplomat, statesman, soldier, all in one. That he was measurably successful in these tasks is the basis of his claim to rank among the great statesmen of modern times.

For the moment his most pressing task was to keep

the English throne. Scotland and Ireland were in revolt, and in England itself there was a mass of dis-
affection which at the least opportunity might turn into
active disloyalty. The critical point for the time being
was in Ireland, where the whole Catholic population
had risen in favor of James. Louis had seen his opportunity, and within a few weeks after James appeared at Versailles, had sent him to Ireland with
troops and money. The danger was the more pressing
in that the French navy, fostered and built up by Colbert, was at such a point of strength and efficiency as
to be able to challenge the English and Dutch for control of the sea. Thus the English were unable to prevent the French from sending supplies and reinforcements to Ireland, and success there would be but the
prelude to an attempt to invade England and drive
William from the English throne. A decision upon
this issue was reached in the year 1690. William
crossed to Ireland in person with a large force and defeated the Franco-Irish army of James at the decisive
battle of the Boyne (July 1). James retired to France,
and in the course of the following year the revolt in
Ireland was stamped out.

Meantime the diplomatic efforts of William had also
borne fruit in the formation of the Grand Alliance,
completed in the winter of 1689-1690. Arrayed
against France were England, Holland, Austria, Spain,
and Savoy, besides most of the minor German states.
France was a beleaguered fortress, surrounded on all
sides by enemies.

The military situation was, however, not so promising for the allies as it might appear on paper. France
had by far the largest and most efficient army in
Europe led by men, who, if not military geniuses,
were at least more than a match for their opponents.

The French frontiers were protected by a ring of almost impregnable fortresses constructed by the great military engineer Vauban. Organized for war as was no other European state, France was able to assume the offensive and to fight her wars largely on foreign soil, thus avoiding the devastation of her territory and the consequent depletion of her resources.

William, on the other hand, was the head of an ill-assorted coalition. Of the allies Spain was scarce able to defend herself, Savoy would always seek the winning side, Austria was handicapped by a war with the Turks. Germany was a reservoir of men, but with almost no machinery to mobilize its resources. Of Holland alone he could be certain, for his hold upon England was still precarious. Moreover, of the allied states Holland and England alone possessed sufficient financial resources to carry on war on the necessary scale; the other states must be subsidized by the Maritime Powers. If William should lose the support of England with its navy and its financial resources, the coalition would collapse and France would gain a not unfavorable peace.

Louis recognized this fact and prepared to strike another blow at William. For the year 1692 he planned a double offensive, one attack in the Netherlands to keep the Dutch and Germans fully occupied, and one against England itself. The French fleet under Tourville, which had won a great victory in 1690 over the Anglo-Dutch fleet at Beachy Head, was still able to keep the sea against its opponents. Louis now ordered Tourville to clear the Channel for an invasion of England. The French admiral attempted to obey, but was decisively beaten at La Hogue by a much superior Anglo-Dutch force. This was the end of the French naval threat. With no special interest in the navy, and finding that the continental conflict was fast consuming his resources, Louis neglected his fleet. Major operations were abandoned in favor of a war of commerce-destroying. Vessels of the navy were loaned to successful commerce-destroyers like Jean Bart and Duguay-Trouin, whose operations in this war have placed their names in the history of the French navy beside those of men like Tourville, De Grasse, and Suffren.

The centre of operations now shifted to the continent. In the Netherlands, though several times beaten, William maintained himself with a stubborn courage which denied the French any decisive victory. Louis then sought to break up the coalition by detaching Spain and Savoy, counting upon his control of the Mediterranean to give him success. It was here that William made an important contribution to the strategy of the Anglo-French wars. In 1694 a strong Anglo-Dutch fleet was sent to the Mediterranean, and against the wishes of its commander was forced to winter there. The French plan of campaign was thus frustrated by the use of naval power, and the English learned the strategic importance of the Mediterranean. When the English fleet was withdrawn, the Duke of Savoy was induced to make peace with France and the French were able to take Barcelona, but too late to affect the outcome of the war.

The first Anglo-French war, like all those which followed it, became a contest of endurance. Such was the balance of forces that a military decision proved impossible. For such a struggle the Maritime Powers had certain marked advantages. Although severally inferior in national wealth to France, they had a greater portion of their wealth in fluid form, their systems of finance were sound, and their national credit

was good. The absurdly unequal system of taxation in
France, which threw almost the whole burden upon
the poverty-stricken peasantry, and the lack of a
sound banking system, which made it difficult to
mobilize the national resources, were among the major
causes of France's lack of success.

In such a contest maritime superiority was also a
great asset, and the two sea powers were not slow to
use it in all possible ways. Although largely self-sufficing, France was a great commercial nation, a rival of
England and Holland. With the double object of put-
ting economic pressure upon France and of ruining a
commercial rival England and Holland agreed in 1689
to prevent both their own nationals and neutrals from
trading with France. The results of this attempt at a
continental blockade appear to have been unsatisfactory, but in the game of commerce-destroying the
Maritime Powers had a great advantage. Although the
French privateers, swarming from the Channel ports,
captured an extraordinary number of English and
Dutch merchantmen, they were unable seriously to
cripple English and Dutch trade. The Maritime
Powers, on the other hand, as the war progressed, were
able to sweep the French merchant marine from the
sea, to cut off the French overseas trade, and thus to
contribute to the growing exhaustion of France.

In one respect, however, William was at a disadvan-
tage in carrying on a long war,—he was not like Louis
XIV, an absolute monarch. It was necessary for him
to secure the consent and co-operation of his subjects
both in Holland and England. So long as they lay
directly in the path of French ambitions William's
Dutch subjects could not afford to quarrel with him.
Once the English felt secure from French attack, however, they were likely to be of two minds about carry-

ing on a long and costly continental war. Of the two parties which divided the political allegiance of Englishmen the Tories, representative of the landed classes which bore the brunt of taxation, were generally opposed to a costly continental war. The Whigs, however, were more favorable. As the champions of Parliamentary supremacy, they were far more concerned than the Tories to prevent a Stuart restoration. Representing the financial and commercial interests, they felt more keenly the effects of French commercial rivalry. To prevent the return of James and to weaken a commercial rival the Whigs were willing to support William and his policy of a continental war. The results of this alliance were momentous. Not only was one of the two great parties committed to William's foreign policy, but William, with the aid of Whig financiers, was able to carry out a financial reorganization which greatly increased the ability of England to stand the strain of this and future wars. It was at this time that the currency was reformed, the system of taxation revised, and the borrowing power of the government greatly expanded by the establishment of the Bank of England. These Whig financial achievements are to be accounted not the least among the causes of the ultimate victory of England in the war.

The conflict in the colonies was no more decisive than that in Europe. Neither government was able to spare forces for large scale colonial enterprises. Save in the West Indies, therefore, where operations necessarily depended upon naval power, the American colonists were left to fight out their own quarrels. The French of Canada, impoverished and reduced to extremities by the raids of the Iroquois, fought gladly, knowing that it was a question of their existence.

Large sections of the population of New York and New England were sufficiently irritated against the French, for reasons already discussed, to be willing to fight. But the more southerly colonies, feeling no danger and no conflict of interest, were content to remain passive spectators of a contest in which they were officially, but not actually, involved. The French government gave such assistance as it could. The English government, knowing the enormous numerical superiority of the English colonists, saw no reason why they should not only defend themselves, but conquer Canada.

Throughout the war it was the more warlike French who forced the pace. At the outset the French government sent over the veteran Frontenac, ablest of the governors of New France, to restore the situation. To reanimate his native allies and to restore the courage of the French, Frontenac undertook a series of raids upon the English settlements. Begun under special circumstances, these raids soon became the characteristic form of French military effort in America. They enabled the French to make the most of their small forces, provided the Indian allies of France with a congenial occupation, kept the English on the defensive, and prevented the further expansion of their settlements. The immediate advantages were certainly all in favor of the French. Nevertheless, the wisdom of such a policy has been questioned by no less an authority than Parkman. Left to themselves, the unwarlike English colonies, as he points out, might have preferred to remain neutral in the contest of the home governments. French and Indian raids, however, kept alive their hatred of the French, stimulated them to attempt reprisals, and resulted in continual appeals to the English government for assistance in the conquest of Canada. Long before the English government was ready to attempt such an operation, the northern English colonies were convinced that their only hope of safety lay in the destruction of the French power in Canada.

Frontenac's first raids produced an immediate response on the part of the English colonies. Encouraged by the Iroquois to take the offensive, they arranged for a concerted effort against the French colonies. A force from Boston easily reduced the French colony of Acadia, and later in the same year (1690) a combined land and sea expedition was despatched against Quebec. It speedily appeared, however, that the difficulties in the way of a conquest of Canada were greater than the English colonies, with their own small resources, could overcome. Exhausted by these efforts, the English were thrown back on the defensive.

The remainder of the war in America was marked by a series of French successes. Acadia was recovered, the New England frontier was devastated, and many settlements were broken up. The New England fisheries were all but destroyed, and its commerce seriously crippled by French privateers. A destructive French raid upon Newfoundland added to the discomfort of the English. New York, protected by the Iroquois, suffered less in material damage, but was equally exhausted.

It was the growing exhaustion of both parties which finally brought the war to a conclusion. The French began to feel the effects of so stupendous a conflict as early as 1693, but were not yet ready to offer satisfactory terms of peace. In 1697, however, William arranged terms of peace with the French at Ryswick. While in general the *status quo ante* was restored, in reality the peace marked a serious check to the ambitions of the French king. Louis was forced to acknowledge William as King of England, to permit the Dutch, as a guarantee against sudden attack, to garrison a string of fortresses along the border of the Spanish Netherlands, to restore all his continental acquisitions since the peace of Nimwegen (1678) except Strasburg. The calculations of William had proved correct. The weight of England, thrown into the scale on the anti-French side, had restored the balance of power.

Scarcely had peace been signed when a new and far more serious threat to the balance of power appeared, for the question of the disposition of the vast Spanish inheritance must soon be decided. The death of the last male of the Spanish Hapsburg house, long awaited, was now imminent. In Europe Spain still ruled the Spanish Netherlands, Milan, and Naples; in America her colonial empire was virtually intact. The principal claimants to the inheritance were the Austrian Hapsburgs, and Louis XIV, whose mother and wife had both been princesses of Spain. To permit either claimant to secure the whole inheritance would upset the balance of power in Europe; to permit France to add the Spanish colonial empire to that which she already possessed would also destroy the maritime balance of power. Louis XIV recognized this fact and consented to negotiate with William III on the basis of a division of the inheritance. At the same time he permitted his ambassador at Madrid to endeavor to secure from the King of Spain a will leaving the whole inheritance to his second grandson, Philip of Anjou. Thus it came about that when William and Louis had already concluded a treaty of partition, the dying King of Spain signed a will in favor of the Duke of Anjou.

Louis hesitated which course to pursue, but influenced largely by the fact that neither the English nor the Dutch seemed disposed to support William in a war to keep Philip from the Spanish throne, decided to accept the will. Had Louis contented himself with seating his grandson upon the throne of Spain, war might have been avoided, but by raising other issues Louis made it possible for William to arouse the English and Dutch people against him. By seizing the Barrier Fortresses assigned to them by the treaty of Ryswick, the French king alarmed the Dutch; by securing from his grandson special privileges for French merchants in the Spanish colonies, he aroused both Maritime Powers; by recognizing the son of James II as James III of England, he outraged English sentiment. Assured now of support William recreated the Grand Alliance, the terms of which stipulated that Austria was to secure a share of the Spanish possessions in Europe, while England and Holland were to keep such conquests as they might make in the New World.

At this point William III died (1702), but in John Churchill, Duke of Marlborough, he left a successor more than equal to the task of carrying on his work. Secure in the favor of the new English sovereign, Anne, through the latter's friendship with his wife, and possessing the entire confidence of the ministry, Marlborough was assured of a support at home which had sometimes been denied to William. As a diplomat he was William's equal, as a soldier immeasurably his superior, for he was perhaps the greatest soldier England has produced. In the great Austrian commander, Prince Eugene, he had a most efficient collaborator.

In some respects, however, the position of the French was more favorable than it had been in 1689. Spain was now on the side of France, and Spanish ports were closed to the allies. The Spanish Netherlands passed into French hands without a blow; the Mediterranean appeared to be a Bourbon lake. In Germany

the Electors of Bavaria and Cologne adhered to France.
The friendship of the former threw open the Danube
valley for a direct advance upon Vienna, that of the
latter afforded a convenient route for the invasion of
Holland. At the outset Savoy and Portugal also in-
clined to the side of France.

The obvious move for the French was to keep Marlborough and the Dutch occupied in the Netherlands
while they struck at Vienna, much as Napoleon did in
1805, with the hope of forcing Austria to make a separate peace. Thus the coalition might be broken up.
But Marlborough divined their plans and, advancing
rapidly across central Germany, joined forces with
Prince Eugene on the Danube, thus interposing a
strong force between the French and Vienna.   The
utter rout of the French at Blenheim (August, 1704)
was the decisive battle of the war. Austria was saved,
the coalition cemented, the eventual success of the allies assured.

It was now possible for the English to consider what
direction they would give to the war, whether to fight a
maritime and colonial war, or to concentrate their ac-
tivities upon the continent. The legacy of William
III, the wishes of England's continental allies, and the
personal preferences of Marlborough, who for a time
after Blenheim enjoyed an unbounded authority, told
heavily in favor of the latter policy. To cripple France
and to prevent the union of France and Spain seemed
the surest guarantees of the balance of power. Thus
while Marlborough, by a series of splendid victories,
cleared the Netherlands and drove the French back
upon their own frontier, the allies also embarked upon
a contest to drive Louis' grandson from the throne of
Spain. This had been no part of the original plan of
the Grand Alliance, but was entered upon tentatively in

1703 to secure the alliance of Portugal. Soon, however, it became in the eyes of the war party in England, and especially of the Whigs, the principal objective of the war.

A long and exhausting struggle now ensued in and around the Spanish peninsula, maintained largely by English armies, in which the decisive factor was the total refusal of the greater part of Spain to accept a king forced upon them by foreign arms. What Napoleon could not accomplish a century later, the English with far smaller resources could not do at this time. Though unsuccessful in their main objective, the English did establish themselves as a Mediterranean power by the capture of Gibraltar (1704) and Minorca (1708), and thus assured themselves adequate naval bases in that sea.

Everywhere, in fact, but in Spain, the allies secured the ascendency, and in Spain itself the province of Catalonia adhered to their cause. At sea the French were scarcely capable of any sustained effort except commerce-destroying. France was soon utterly exhausted, and Louis XIV sought peace. In the abortive peace negotiations of 1709-1710 Louis offered to abandon the cause of his grandson, and to do everything, in fact, which the allies demanded except to join them in driving Philip from Spain. Thus the disposition of Spain became the chief barrier to peace. At this juncture the insistence of the Whig party, which was now in power in England, on continuing the war until Philip was expelled, produced a reaction in that country. In 1710 the Whigs were driven from power, and their Tory successors took steps to end the war. Meantime, however, in accordance with their principles, the Tories sought to emphasize the colonial side of the struggle, which hitherto had been neglected.

At the outset of the second war the French government, conscious of its maritime weakness, favored the maintenance of neutrality in America. The local French authorities, fearful of the Iroquois, so far complied as to promise the latter not to attack New York if they would abstain from attacking Canada. As regards New England, however, they felt it necessary to stir the Abnaki to war, lest the English win them over, and the New England frontier again became the scene of French and Indian raids. Thus while New York remained at peace, war raged on the frontiers of New England and Acadia. The adhesion of Spain to the side of France, and the French settlement of Louisiana in 1699, involved the southernmost English colony of South Carolina also in the conflict. Thus again America became the scene of an Anglo-French war.

The results of the first war had convinced English officials in America that only with English assistance could the colonies free themselves of the French menace. But the war in Spain had so far consumed English resources that it was not until 1709 that the government could be persuaded to promise a force for an attack upon Canada. At the last moment, however, the promised armament was diverted to Portugal, and so long as the Whigs were in office the sole result of repeated colonial appeals for aid was the despatch, in 1710, of a small force which reduced Acadia.

The chiefs of the new Tory ministry, Harley and St. John (Bolingbroke), at once took steps to show their interest in the colonies. In 1711 Harley formed a South Sea Company to exploit the trade of the Caribbean and considered the despatch of an expedition to make conquests from the French and Spanish in that area. St. John took up with great zeal the idea of conquering

Canada, but the imposing expedition which he sent in 1711 was grossly mismanaged and failed miserably.

Meantime, in violation of the terms of the Grand Alliance, the Tory government was engaged in secret peace negotiations with the French. Believing, or professing to believe, that the allies were selfishly using English resources to accomplish ends in which England had no real interest, the ministry made a separate peace, known as the peace of Utrecht (1713). This peace is the first great landmark in the Second Hundred Years' War. The Spanish inheritance was divided, Spain and the Indies remaining in the hands of Philip V, the remainder, with slight exceptions, going to Austria. The balance of power was restored, more as a result of the exhaustion of all the powers than of the terms of the treaty itself. The acquisition of Gibraltar and Minorca made England a great Mediterranean power, and gave her ample opportunity to counteract French influence in that quarter. France was forced to banish the Stuarts, to recognize the rights of the House of Hanover to the English throne, and to demolish Dunkirk, the chief French base for commerce-destroying. The cession of the Spanish Netherlands to Austria, and the retention by Holland of the Barrier Fortresses, insured that important area against any sudden French attack.

The colonial settlement was less favorable to England, but corresponded equally well to the facts of the situation. Spain granted to England the famous Asiento, or contract to supply the Spanish colonies with slaves, together with the right to send yearly to the Spanish colonies one trading ship of not over five hundred tons burden. France ceded to England Acadia, Newfoundland, and the Hudson's Bay territory, and in a vaguely worded clause acknowledged English suzerainty over the Iroquois. Despite the warnings of men familiar with America, however, the ministry, in its haste to conclude peace, made concessions which largely nullified the effect of these gains. The French were allowed to keep the island of Cape Breton, where they soon reared the fortress of Louisbourg to command the mouth of the St. Lawrence, and to take the place of Port Royal as a base for their fishermen and their privateers. They were also permitted to fish about the coast of Newfoundland and to dry fish on its shores. No serious attempt was made to settle the question of colonial boundaries, for the contest for colonial supremacy was in its initial stages, and the decisive conflict for America was yet to come.

One other result of this war demands notice. Before it, says Admiral Mahan, "England was one of the sea powers; after it she was *the* sea power, without any second." Exhausted by long wars, Holland had fallen behind her larger, more populous, and better organized rivals. The sea power of France had been temporarily destroyed and her commerce swept from the seas. Perhaps the greatest advantage which England drew from the war was the fact that her strength was unimpaired, and that she was in the best position to profit from the period of peace which followed.

For thirty years following the peace of Utrecht England and France remained at peace. Although commercial and colonial rivalry continued, the balance of power had been restored, and both powers were too exhausted to seek an immediate renewal of the conflict. Moreover, the domestic situation in both counselled peace, and even led to the conclusion of an Anglo-French alliance. In France, following the death of Louis XIV (1715), the government devolved upon the Duke of Orleans as Regent for the young Louis XV. The principal concern of Orleans was to protect his rights as next in line of succession to the throne against Philip of Spain, whose prior rights had been set aside by the peace of Utrecht. In England the accession of the House of Hanover, following the death of Anne (1714), gave the Whigs a long lease of power. Friendship with France was no part of their original creed, but circumstances forced them to reconsider their policy. Their primary object was to establish their own power and the position of the House of Hanover by preventing a Stuart restoration. Only with the support of France would the Stuarts be dangerous, hence the desirability of conciliating France. A second important consideration was the protection of Hanover, now joined to England by a personal union. To all intents and purposes England had ceased to be an insular power; her diplomacy and her strategy must be governed accordingly. On the basis, therefore, of a mutual guarantee of the position of the House of Orleans and the House of Hanover a Triple Alliance was formed in 1717 consisting of England, France, and Holland. At the same time Whig statesmen sought to preserve the friendship of Austria. Thus for a few years England dominated continental politics.

Such a condition of affairs could not be lasting. Among Whig statesmen there was a difference of opinion concerning the degree to which England should allow herself to be involved in continental affairs. Some were prepared to intervene on every occasion, believing that England's commercial interests alone, exclusive of the question of the balance of power, necessitated a continual watchfulness concerning European developments. Others, of whom Robert Walpole was chief, argued that England would do better to keep the peace and to develop her trade unless some major crisis should arise.

Hence when Walpole came to dominate English foreign policy, about 1730, England for a time abstained from active intervention.

The French, for their part, could not remain content to submit to English leadership and to play a secondary rôle in continental affairs. The aged, but capable, Cardinal Fleury, who governed France from 1726 to 1743, strove quietly and successfully to reassert French leadership on the continent by cultivating the friendship of Spain and by reviving the traditional French hostility for the House of Austria. The renewal of Franco-Hapsburg rivalry in the War of Polish Succession (1733-1738) put a great strain upon Anglo-French friendship, but as long as Fleury abstained from reviving the territorial ambitions of Louis XIV, as long above all as he did not disturb the *status quo* in the Low Countries, Walpole was content to maintain peace. Nevertheless, the Anglo-French alliance was seriously weakened.

In other respects, also, the policies of Walpole and Fleury made the continuance of Anglo-French friendship more difficult. Both were assiduous in promoting the commercial development of their respective countries. The rapid recovery of France after defeat has been a marked feature of her history, and, as in the time of Colbert, so now, the appearance of strong French competition in certain branches of trade aroused the serious apprehensions of the English commercial classes. Statistics, if available, would probably show that England's commercial advance was even more rapid than that of France, but in their jealousy the English attributed to the French a design of "pushing into an universal commerce, as the surer, though slower, way of coming at their old darling scheme of universal dominion."

In the colonies Anglo-French rivalry continued un-abated. The French carried far towards completion their scheme of securing the interior of North America with a network of forts and Indian alliances, and per-haps the most significant development of the period is the awakening of Pennsylvania and Virginia to the threat to their interests implied in this policy. Mean-while French success in gaining over a portion of the Iroquois, and French support of the Abnaki in the war which they fought with Massachusetts from 1721 to 1726, served to keep alive the enmity of New York and New England. Beyond an occasional protest, however, the British government took no notice of these develop-ments, and in truth the increasing disparity in wealth and numbers between the British and French colonies gave the latter quite as much cause for anxiety as the former.

It was a commercial dispute which brought to an end the period of peace. In no quarter had the English been more active in pushing their trade since the peace of Utrecht than in the Spanish colonies. Their high-handed methods in attempting to break down the Span-ish monopoly aroused the just resentment of the Span-ish government, which, under the Bourbons, was con-ducted with more efficiency and vigor than formerly. Reprisals followed, to be greeted in England by an ex-plosion of popular wrath, which drove the government into an undesired war. Aware of the increasingly friendly relations of the French and Spanish courts, and fearful that war with Spain would soon be followed by war with France, Walpole strove in vain to preserve peace.

While Anglo-French relations were strained by this so-called War of Jenkins' Ear (Jenkins was an English captain whose ear had supposedly been cut off in a fray with a Spanish *guarda costa*), the actual rupture was produced by the sudden appearance of a new threat to the balance of power. In 1740, the year following the outbreak of the Anglo-Spanish war, the Emperor Charles VI died, leaving his possessions to his daughter, Maria Theresa. Although her rights of succession had been solemnly guaranteed by all the Great Powers, the chance to weaken the House of Austria was one which, in that cynical age, the statesmen of Europe could not resist. When the sudden attack of Frederick of Prussia revealed the weakness of the Hapsburg monarchy, the war party at the French court forced the hand of the aged Fleury, and France joined a coalition of powers to partition the Hapsburg possessions.

England now became involved in this War of the Austrian Succession, not merely as the ally of Austria, but as the chief guardian of the balance of power, for if Austria were partitioned by her enemies, there would cease to be on the continent any great military power to serve as a counterpoise to France. In this crisis it was the policy of Walpole to assist in the preservation of Austria merely by the use of financial and diplomatic means, but after his fall, in 1742, the English government allowed itself to be drawn into a war of revenge, fought by Austria with English assistance against the Bourbon powers. From being a mere auxiliary, England became a principal in the war, which now developed into a conflict of rival coalitions along the lines of the War of the Spanish Succession, England, Holland, Austria, and Sardinia on the one side, France and Spain on the other. War was officially declared against France in the spring of 1744.

The ensuing war is the most tedious and the least interesting of all the Anglo-French wars. Becoming involved in war with one another in this indirect fashion the English and French statesmen of the time were unable to fix upon a definite objective in their mutual combat. It was already clear that Austria was not to be partitioned, hence the balance of power ceased to be in question. Some in England, notably the young William Pitt, argued that England should abandon the continental war and strike for colonial and commercial supremacy, but the older politicians were incapable of such a violent readjustment of policy.

The war, therefore, was fought on the old familiar lines, with Austrian and Sardinian armies fighting the French and Spanish in Italy, Austrian armies guarding the Rhine, and English and Dutch armies striving to keep the French out of the Netherlands. English efforts on the continent were seriously hampered for a time by the romantic attempt of the Stuart Pretender to regain the throne of his ancestors, but his defeat at Culloden (1746) marked the end of the tragedy which began in 1688, and effectively removed the question of the English succession from the arena of Anglo-French politics. Even after his defeat the English had no success in checking the celebrated Marshal Saxe, who overran the Austrian Netherlands and threatened to invade Holland. To redress the balance upon the continent the English government negotiated to secure the aid of Russia, but this proved unnecessary. The balance had already been redressed by the English fleet, which had driven the French merchant marine from the sea, and had virtually destroyed their fighting fleet. In Italy also the Bourbon arms had been unsuccessful. In the colonial conflict the English capture of Louisbourg was counterbalanced by their loss of Madras in India. An exhausting and purposeless war was now concluded by an unsatisfactory peace.

The peace of Aix-la-Chapelle (1748) restored the

status quo ante in the colonies. In Europe France agreed to retire from the Netherlands in return for an Italian principality for the son-in-law of Louis XV, who was one of the younger Spanish Bourbons. The chief cost of the war was borne by Austria, which had to confirm the cession of Silesia to Prussia and yield part of the duchy of Milan to Sardinia. Forgetful of the fact that English assistance had saved her from a far worse fate, Maria Theresa complained that the English alliance had brought her nothing but losses. To express their dissatisfaction the French coined a proverb, *Bête comme la paix* (As stupid as the peace). In England the elder statesmen congratulated themselves on escaping so well, while the young Pitt bided his time. The time had come when Europe was to recede from the centre of the stage, and when English and French statesmen alike would see in the colonies the true path to empire.

CHAPTER II

THE CONTEST FOR COLONIAL SUPREMACY
(1748-1763)

The peace of Aix-la-Chapelle (1748) marks the end of one phase of the Anglo-French conflict. In the three wars fought since 1689 European questions, questions of dynastic succession, of the balance of power, had been uppermost. Commercial rivalry was a factor, but colonial rivalry had played a distinctly subordinate part. It was the third war which revealed, particularly to English statesmen, the character and importance of the colonial conflict, and now that the continental balance was not seriously in question, they were free to orient English policy accordingly. The period between the third and fourth wars is the period when this reorientation was gradually taking place. The fourth war was the result not of European questions but of colonial rivalries.

Both in America and in India the struggle of the two nations continued despite the conclusion of the European peace. Up to the beginning of the third Anglo-French war the English and French had confined themselves in India to commercial operations. Both countries had organized East India companies to carry on their eastern trade. The English company, established in 1600, was perhaps the strongest and wealthiest commercial organization in England and had large political influence, since many of its directors and stockholders had seats in Parliament. The chief English trading centres, or factories, in India were Madras on the southeast coast, Bombay on the west, and Calcutta in the delta of the Ganges. The French company was a far weaker organization. Save for a period of about twenty years, from 1720 to 1740, it never prospered financially, and it was completely dependent for support upon the French government, which appointed its directors. The principal French factories were Pondicherry, a little south of Madras, and Chandernagore, near Calcutta.

So long as India was ruled by a strong native power, the Europeans carried on their commercial operations more or less on sufferance. From 1526 to 1707 India was largely controlled by a line of Mongol conquerors, descended from the great Tamerlane, who had their capital at Delhi. Their power was greatest in the vast plain of northern India, but even in the south most of the local rulers, whether Hindu or Mohammedan, acknowledged their suzerainty. India was certainly not a nation, nor was it a well organized state judged by European standards, but down to 1707 the Mogul emperors were able to enforce their will throughout the greater part of the country. It was from them that the Europeans had secured trade concessions.

In 1707 the last able ruler of the Mogul line, Aurangzeb by name, died, and the Mogul empire underwent that rapid process of disintegration which is the fate of all Oriental empires when the ruling house decays. Even during the reign of Aurangzeb a strong Hindu power, the Marathas, had arisen on the west coast, east of Bombay, and after his death the various local rulers and viceroys, who had once recognized the imperial authority, began to set up for themselves. The condition of India after the death of Aurangzeb was like that of Europe after the death of Charlemagne, when various feudal states were taking form. The invasion of the Persian Nadir Shah in 1739 may be said to

have completed the ruin of the Mogul power. Thenceforth the power of the emperor was as shadowy as
that of the later Merovingians.

Sooner or later probably the growing anarchy in
India would have forced the European commercial
organizations operating there to seek some territorial
basis for their power. The crisis in India, which
brought that country into the Anglo-French conflict for
commercial empire, was, however, precipitated by the
activity of Joseph François Dupleix, who became Di-
rector-General of the French Company in India in
1742. It was formerly believed that from the first
Dupleix set himself to establish the French as a territorial power in India and to ruin their English rivals.
It is probably a truer view to conceive of these objects
as taking shape in his mind gradually as favorable op-
portunities presented themselves. It is known that
when, in 1742, the French government sought to make
an agreement with the English East India Company for
the maintenance of neutrality in the East in case of war,
Dupleix approved of the idea, and that it was the English Company, which, hoping to use English naval
power to destroy the trade of its rival, refused to come
to an agreement.

Even before war broke out between England and
France in 1744, Dupleix and his predecessor, Dumas,
had laid the foundations of a new policy by gaining the
friendship of the chief local potentate, the Nawab of
the Carnatic, in which district both Madras and Pondicherry are situated. When news of war reached India,
each company prepared to attack its rival, but the
value of native friendship was illustrated when the
Nawab forbade the English to attack Pondicherry.
The next year (1746), Dupleix, with the assistance
of a French squadron from the Isle of France, the

French naval base in the East, took Madras, and when the Nawab demanded that it be turned over to him, taught him a sharp lesson by inflicting a severe defeat upon his forces. This victory, gained by European-trained and armed native troops (sepoys), demonstrated to native and European alike the immense superiority of such a force over the native armies, and encouraged Dupleix to undertake a more active policy.

The peace of 1748 restored, ostensibly, the *status quo ante* in India, but the war had left the French and English suspicious of one another. It had also encouraged Dupleix to pursue further his schemes, and, by leaving him with a considerable force of reliable troops, gave him the means for so doing. An opportunity now presented itself in the outbreak of a double succession contest in the neighboring native states. The ranking potentate of southern India, who ruled nominally as the imperial viceroy, was the Nizam of Hyderabad. On the death of the ruling Nizam in 1748 a struggle broke out over the succession. In the same year a similar contest over the succession arose in the Carnatic, whose Nawab was a vassal of the Nizam. Dupleix saw an opportunity, by supporting one pretender against another in these two native states, to establish himself solidly in the favor of the principal native princes of southern India, and to strike a blow at the position of the English without making a direct attack upon them.

The similarity of French policy in India and America will be noted. In both the French schemes depended upon asserting their military superiority over their European rivals, and upon this basis establishing their influence over the natives. War and diplomacy had gained France her position in Europe; it was natural to assume that they could do likewise in India or America. The weak point in the French scheme, as all

writers have pointed out, was that the resources to carry
on such a policy must be drawn, for a long time at
least, from France, and that, therefore, the maintenance of an uninterrupted communication with the
home base, in war as well as in peace, was essential to
its success. "The last word," it has been said, "lay
with sea power."

The English were not blind to the danger of letting
Dupleix succeed, and found themselves compelled to
imitate his policy. Consequently they also, rather tim-
idly at first, adopted the cause of rival pretenders. For
a time it appeared that their intervention was too late.
Dupleix established his candidate firmly on the throne
of Hyderabad, under the tutelage and protection of an
able officer, Bussy. In the Carnatic the English candidate, by 1751, retained but a single fortress where he
was closely besieged by a French and native force. It
was at this low ebb in their fortunes that the English
were rescued by the extraordinary genius of a young
clerk in the employ of the East India Company, Robert
Clive. By seizing Arcot, the capital of the Carnatic,
and holding it against unbelievable odds Clive created
a diversion which marked a turn in the tide. Within a
short time the French had been defeated, their candidate for the Carnatic slain, and the English candidate duly established as Nawab. Dupleix was still
sanguine of ultimate success, but the Company at home
was appalled at the expense of his policy and he was
recalled in 1754, just as a new Anglo-French war was
about to begin. It is probably a too dramatic version
of events which represents the policy of Dupleix as
threatening the entire destruction of English trade and
influence in India. The real significance of Dupleix lies
in the fact that he was the first clearly to attempt to
found the European position in India on territorial

power, and that thereby he set the feet of the English upon the path from which they emerged as masters of all India. Sooner or later probably circumstances would have forced the English to adopt some such policy, but there is every reason to believe that but for Dupleix that time would have been indefinitely postponed.

If the Anglo-French conflict was the more dramatic in India, it was America which occupied the attention of the British and French governments. The despatches of colonial governors, the growing volume of American trade, and the writings of travellers and publicists had aroused the British and French to some appreciation of the importance of the colonies. On both sides it was assumed that the peace was only a truce, and that at the first opportunity each would attempt to destroy the power of its rival in America. In the French system of forts and Indian alliances linking Canada and Louisiana, the English saw a premeditated scheme of barring them from the interior as the first step towards the complete conquest of the English colonies. The French were equally sure that English territorial claims and the westward expansion of the English colonies were but so many steps towards driving them from the American continent. Both firmly believed that they were acting on the defensive.

Moreover, it had become much more than a question of the security of the colonies of England and France in America. The colonies were now regarded as worth fighting for. To men like Shirley and William Pitt the mastery of America carried with it commercial and naval predominance. The power which controlled its fish, its furs, its sugar, would control the commerce of the world. Its fisheries were an unequalled nursery for seamen, and its naval stores afforded the basis for an indefinite expansion of the navy and the merchant marine. And proceeding further along this line, it was argued, by French and English writers alike, that the power which could monopolize the wealth of America would be able to gain the mastery in Europe. Thus the preservation of the balance of power in Europe was held to depend upon the preservation of a balance of power in America. If that were so, and it was increasingly accepted as true, the time had come when America must take a foremost place in the plans of European diplomats and statesmen.

When such was the state of mind of the two rivals, the establishment of peace in Europe could have little effect upon the conflict in America. The war had revealed to each the weakness of its position and the necessity of strengthening the weak places before the inevitable next war. The French were particularly on the alert, since, as the Governor of Canada pointed out, owing to the weakness of French naval power, the reinforcement of Canada in time of war was by no means assured.

At two points in particular the conflict was acute in the years of nominal peace which intervened between the third and fourth wars. The first of these was Acadia, which had been nominally an English possession since the peace of Utrecht. Unfortunately for them, the English had done little more to maintain their possession than to keep a governor and a small garrison at Annapolis, the former Port Royal. The French population, now grown to ten or twelve thousand, remained, under the influence of their priests, passively hostile to English rule. The people were simple and ignorant and desired only to be let alone, but in times of conflict some of them openly manifested their hostility to the English by assisting in French attacks.

The Indians of Acadia, under the influence of French missionaries, made no pretence of accepting English rule and were, at most times, actively hostile.

The war awakened both French and English to the unsatisfactory state of affairs. Acadia itself was regarded as of little importance, save that it was considered by both sides as a valuable base of operations against Louisbourg and Canada, and that its possession by the French was a standing menace to New England. Furthermore, its boundaries were in dispute. The English asserted, following earlier French claims, that it included the whole region between the Kennebec and the St. Lawrence. The French maintained that Acadia was only the peninsula, now known as Nova Scotia. As a step towards making good their claims they established themselves, shortly after the peace, at the neck of the isthmus, where they built a fort which served as a base for Indian depredations upon the English, and as a centre for intrigues among the French inhabitants. When the English attempted also to build a fort at the isthmus, the French forcibly, though unsuccessfully, resisted. The chief English accomplishment was to establish a considerable settlement at Halifax in 1749, with the idea of strengthening their hold by increasing the number of English settlers. "In Europe," wrote the Governor of Acadia, "they may observe the Treaty and be at Peace, but here the War is continual & carry'd on by all open and secret means of Violence and Treason."

Even more serious, from the English standpoint, was the situation on the upper Ohio. Largely for fear of offending the Iroquois, who claimed the country north of the Ohio as part of their domain, the French had paid little attention to this natural route between the Lakes and the Mississippi. No sooner had peace been concluded, however, than the French determined to assert their claims to the Ohio country, and a formal expedition was sent in 1749 to take possession in the name of the French king. French disquiet was further increased by the evidence, which this expedition found, of the activity of English traders in the Ohio country and of the friendliness of the Indian tribes of that region for the English. In this same year a group of prominent Virginians and British merchants, organized as the Ohio Company, secured a large grant of land south of the upper Ohio with the design of settling the country and developing the fur trade. This was something more than a land-jobbing scheme, for it had the support of the energetic Governor Dinwiddie of Virginia and of the British Board of Trade, and was regarded as a step towards establishing English claims to the interior and towards blocking French schemes of dominating that area.

A contest now ensued between the Ohio Company and the French for the possession of the Ohio. The latter not only drove the English traders out of the Ohio country, killing the most influential pro-English chief of the region, but began a chain of forts designed to connect Lake Erie with the forks of the Ohio, where Pittsburgh now stands. Alarmed by these measures, Governor Dinwiddie sent a small force to build a fort at the forks, but it was speedily driven off by the French, who built there a fort called Fort Duquesne. Dinwiddie still persisted, and despatched a larger force under the youthful Washington to dislodge the French. After driving off a French detachment with considerable loss, Washington was surrounded by a much larger force of French and Indians and forced to surrender on July 4, 1754. At this point the conflict passed out of the jurisdiction of the local authorities to become the concern of the home governments. The blood shed on the Upper Ohio marks the beginning of the fourth Anglo-French war.

England was at this time governed by a coalition of various Whig factions under the nominal leadership of the Duke of Newcastle. The timid fussiness of Newcastle and his ignorance of colonial affairs have become proverbial, but the long possession of power had given him a wide knowledge of English and European affairs, and in Granville, the former Carteret, and the Earl of Hardwicke he had able advisors. Since the last war the navy had been improved by Anson, who was Hardwicke's son-in-law, and the Duke of Cumberland, a younger son of George II, had introduced certain reforms into the army. The ministry was determined to check French aggression in America, but it was also resolved to avoid a European war. A European war meant the necessity of defending Hanover against the French and a heavy increase in the burdens of taxation, which might lead to popular discontent and produce unpleasant political consequences. It was decided, therefore, by the ministry to prevent France from moving in Europe by constructing a formidable network of alliances, to bring the American colonies together into a closer union which would permit their great numerical strength to be brought to bear, and to send a body of European troops to America, which, with the aid of colonial forces, might drive the French from certain positions recently occupied by them on what was considered English territory. It was hoped that the other powers would consider this a reprisal for French aggression, a state of quasi-war recognized by public law at that time, and that England would thus avoid the onus of beginning an outright war. This was the more to be desired as Spain had a defensive alliance with

France, and would be drawn into the war in case England made a direct attack. A fight to the finish was by no means contemplated, and it was hoped by the more pacific members of the ministry, at least, that when France had been taught a sufficiently sharp lesson she would be ready to make a reasonable compromise on the question of colonial boundaries.

So deplorable was the condition of France at this time, so divided the counsels of her rulers, and so uncertain her policy that the plans of the English ministry seemed to have a fair chance of success. Louis XV reigned, but did not govern. In so far as France had any directing head at this time it was the king's mistress, Madame de Pompadour, who not only squandered vast sums of money to keep herself and the king amused, money which the almost bankrupt state could ill afford, but who set up and pulled down ministers, chose officers to command the French armies, and decided the most important questions of state. Madame de Pompadour, the king, and most of the ministers were sincerely desirous of peace, but they knew little about the American situation and failed to understand that peace could be maintained only by making concessions to the English in America, or by such a vigorous policy in Europe that England would be deterred from acting in the colonies. France's ally Frederick noted with disgust the strange indifference displayed by the French ministers to the activity of their enemies, a sort of lassitude which seemed to have spread from the king, who was always bored, through the whole administration.

Unfortunately for Newcastle and his plans, there was a strong war party in the English ministry headed by the Duke of Cumberland, the favorite son of George II. Cumberland was at the head of the military establishment and wished to precipitate a general war, which would increase his importance. Newcastle was too timid to resist pressure, and allowed himself to be pushed quite beyond his original program of reprisal into a policy of aggression. When it was learned that the French, having heard of the despatch of English forces to America, were sending reinforcements, it was decided to order Admiral Boscawen to intercept them. The greater part of the French fleet escaped him, but two vessels were captured, whereupon the French broke off diplomatic relations. Shortly after this the British war vessels and privateers were let loose on French shipping, and by the end of the year 1755 French ships to the value of more than a million pounds had been captured, all this before any declaration of war.

At the same time the operations of reprisal in America were under way, and at four points the English attacked the French. The expedition of General Braddock against Fort Duquesne ended in a disastrous rout, which destroyed what was left of English prestige among the Indians, and exposed the frontiers of Pennsylvania and Virginia to the horrors of Indian warfare. The expedition under William Johnson against Crown Point succeeded in beating off a French attack and in establishing an English fort at the southern end of Lake George, but was far from attaining its original objective. A third expedition, under Shirley, designed to conquer Niagara, failed even more dismally. The sole success of the English was to dislodge the French from their forts in Acadia, and to deport and disperse the Acadian French among the English colonies, an event famous in literature and in the annals of historical controversy, but of slight bearing upon the outcome of the war. At every point the plans of Newcastle had broken down. His operations of reprisal had failed, and the position of the English in America had changed only for the worse. As for the hope of avoiding a European war, the events of the summer and autumn of 1755 had rendered it a chimera.

Although hoping to avoid a European war, the English ministry had attempted to prepare for any eventuality by providing a defense for Hanover. They turned first, as a matter of course, to their former allies, Holland and Austria, but neither showed any enthusiasm for guarding Hanover while the English were fighting a maritime war for their own advantage. The government next had recourse to Russia, whose assistance could be secured at a price, and in the autumn of 1755 a treaty was concluded with that power for the defense of Hanover. It was this treaty, says a French historian, designed to prevent a European war, which actually precipitated it, for it was the first step towards what is known as the Diplomatic Revolution.

The way for this change in the diplomatic alignment of the powers had already been prepared by the skilful Austrian diplomat, Kaunitz. Ever since the loss of Silesia to Prussia it had been the principal object of Maria Theresa to recover that province. Kaunitz argued correctly that the alliance of England was of little value in a war against Prussia, and that Austria should seek the alliance of France. The reconciliation of the two powers which had uniformly fought on opposite sides for two hundred and fifty years could not be accomplished in a day, but Kaunitz had succeeded in persuading Madame de Pompadour that an Austrian alliance was desirable. Nevertheless, the French government, in the course of its languid preparations to meet the English attack, sought to renew the Prussian alliance, which was about to expire. It was too late. Learning of the Anglo-Russian treaty, which was directed principally against him, Frederick with characteristic rapidity of decision decided to come to terms with England, which was only too glad to secure this additional guarantee for the security of Hanover. The result was the defensive alliance of Prussia and England, concluded in January, 1756, to protect Germany against foreign invasion.

Frederick was willing, if it were possible, to renew the alliance with France, but the Anglo-Prussian treaty was regarded at Versailles as a slap in the face. Madame de Pompadour now carried the day, and in May, 1756, a defensive alliance was concluded between France and Austria, which stipulated the neutrality of Austria in the Anglo-French war and contained a mutual guarantee of the European possessions of the two powers. In the same month war was declared between France and England. Russia was equally irritated at the Anglo-Prussian treaty, for the Czarina Elizabeth hated Frederick, and was prepared to join Austria in attacking Prussia.

This so-called Reversal of the Alliances was of the greatest significance. It made allies of Austria and France, two powers whose enmity had been one of the fixed principles of European international relations. It gave England as a continental ally the young and vigorous power of Prussia whose territories were conveniently situated for the defense of Hanover. Entered into without due forethought by the French, the Austro-French alliance proved a millstone about their necks, for it involved them in a continental war to recover Silesia for Austria, when their principal efforts should have been put forth in the maritime and colonial struggle. The gains which France could hope for from a successful continental war were as nothing compared to the losses which, during their naval weakness, they were likely to suffer in the colonies.

It may be urged in defense of the French that they did not contemplate a European war. Neither at Paris, nor yet at London and Berlin, was a European war desired. The French alliance, however, and the prospect of an alliance with Russia encouraged the court of Vienna to plan an attack upon Prussia. The Prussian king, convinced that war was inevitable, determined to strike the first blow, and began the war in August, 1756, by the invasion of Saxony. The result was to bring about what he most desired to prevent, a coalition of his enemies. In January, 1757, Russia made an alliance with Austria against him, and in May of the same year, the French government, baited by the promise of the cession of certain towns in the Netherlands to France and the bestowal of the remainder of that country upon Don Philip, the son-in-law of Louis XV, joined the league against Prussia. Sweden also was drawn into the ring of enemies. The Prussian state was to be partitioned and Frederick reduced to the rank of a petty German prince. It should be remembered, in judging the conduct of England towards Frederick in the closing months of the war, that the Anglo-Prussian treaty was purely defensive, and that, having started the war, Frederick technically had no claim upon the assistance of England.

The general situation at the outset of this war seemed unusually favorable to England. Though Holland refused to support England, Spain under the pacific Ferdinand VI decided to remain neutral. England also was relieved of the necessity of defending the Low Countries against French attack. There remained Hanover, the defense of which against the French would admittedly be difficult. But the extraordinary ineptitude for waging war displayed by the Newcastle ministry threatened to cost England such advantages as she possessed. So long had the elder Whig statesmen relied upon the time-consuming processes of diplomacy that they were incapable of acting with vigor and decision in a crisis. The Duke of Cumberland, who controlled the army, was both an inefficient commander and a singularly poor judge of military ability in others. Of General Braddock, appointed by Cumberland to the chief command in America, it was said by one who had long been acquainted with him that he had never been known to do anything but swear, and of two of his successors sent to command in America it was confessed by Cumberland's colleagues in the Cabinet that no one believed them capable of high command. On the other hand, disorganized as the French government was, once war was declared it sprang into extraordinary activity and dealt blow after blow at the enemy.

Both in Europe and America the war went steadily against England. First the French threatened to invade England and produced such a panic that the ministry brought over Hessian and Hanoverian troops for its defense. Under cover of this threat the French struck at Minorca and captured it, in June, 1756, after driving off an English fleet sent to relieve it. For his failure to relieve Minorca the unfortunate Admiral Byng was court-martialled and executed, "pour encourager les autres," according to the witticism of Voltaire. In America, in 1756, the French, under the able leadership of Montcalm, took Oswego, the only English fort on the Great Lakes, and followed this the next year with the capture of Fort William Henry on Lake George. Cumberland went in person to defend Hanover and was so thoroughly beaten by the French that he concluded, in September, 1757, a convention at Closter-Seven by which he undertook to disband his army, thus leaving Hanover to the occupation of the French. "I never yet saw so dreadful a prospect," wrote Lord Chesterfield, and Hardwicke confessed, "I look upon this Nation as upon the brink of Ruin." Frederick also, England's only ally, had been beaten by the Austrians at Kolin and forced to retire from Bohemia, while the Russians and the French pressed upon him from east and west.

At this crisis England was saved by William Pitt. It was now more than twenty years since Pitt had entered Parliament, where from the first he had signalized himself by his eloquence and the vigor of his opposition to the policy of Walpole and Newcastle. From 1746 to 1754 he held a minor place in the ministry, and though often critical of the foreign policy of the government, had been less active in his opposition. The Duke of Newcastle, who feared the power of his eloquence in Parliament, would have been glad to secure his full support, but would not pay the price demanded by Pitt, the office of Secretary of State and a place in the Cabinet, and having come to terms with Henry Fox, next to Pitt the most prominent of the younger statesmen, dismissed Pitt from office in November, 1754.

Pitt bided his time. He would accept no place which did not give him a free hand. He had a supreme self-confidence. "I am sure that I can save this country, and that no one else can," he is reported to have said. The central idea, which burned within him, was that England's vocation lay upon the sea, and that it was within her power to become mistress of the empire of commerce. In Parliament he had thundered, session after session, at the policy of subordinating this supreme object to the defense of Hanover, that "despicable electorate," as he called it, and other continental objects. France was the enemy, let her be absolutely destroyed as a maritime and commercial power, that was his guiding principle. By his attacks upon Hanover he had raised an obstacle to his advancement in the hatred and distrust of the king. Born without the circle of great families which had monopolized power so long, he was not admitted to high office until they had no alternative. The basis of his influence, apart from his eloquence, lay in popular support. The commercial classes of England recognized in him their great champion, and to the last he had their enthusiastic support. The common people also trusted him; he was the Great Commoner. He was the voice of the new England which had been slowly developing during the long peace, which as yet had suffered itself to be governed by a narrow clique of aristocrats. It is not necessary to conceal, or attempt to explain away, Pitt's theatricality or his many inconsistencies; they are the defects of a genius which bordered at times upon insanity. There is much in his earlier and later career to detract from his reputation. It is enough to recognize that he was incorruptible, that he was above the arts of the petty patronage-dispensing politician, that he had the power to arouse an age and a people little given to enthusiasms, and that he was the greatest war minister England ever had. His place among English statesmen rests securely upon the success with which he raised England from the despair of failure and led her to the most complete of all her victories over France.

It was not until the summer of 1757, too late to affect the campaigns of that year, that Pitt secured a free hand. Overwhelmed by the odium of successive defeats Newcastle had resigned in November, 1756, and

Pitt had been called upon to form a ministry. Within a few months, however, he was summarily dismissed by the king, who still distrusted him. A prolonged crisis ensued, which was ended only at the close of June, 1757, by the formation of a coalition of the major political factions. Pitt became Secretary of State with a free hand to direct the war, Newcastle was left at the head of the Treasury where he could dispense patronage, Fox accepted a minor, though lucrative, office. Pitt is said to have remarked that he borrowed the Duke of Newcastle's majority to fight the war.

Until the downfall of Pitt, England had the advantage of such a centralized control of policy and strategy as she has rarely enjoyed. Pitt took complete charge of diplomacy and of the naval and military operations. To Newcastle was left the task of seeing that Parliament appropriated, year after year, money sufficient for the carrying on of the war. In Anson as head of the Admiralty he had an efficient administrator, in Boscawen and Hawke, admirals of proved worth. The army, however, had been badly led, and it is one of the remarkable features of Pitt's genius that he was able to pick capable officers regardless of their age and previous rank, and inspire them with his own confidence in victory. It was Pitt also who gained from the American colonies a degree of coöperation which no other English statesman was able to secure. Year after year he called upon the colonies to levy, pay, and clothe 20,000 men, promising that England would supply them with arms and ammunition, and that he would ask Parliament to reimburse them, in part, for their extraordinary expenses. It was a sign also of Pitt's recognition of the human element that he removed the dissatisfaction of the colonial officers by giving due recognition to their rank. Though Canada was conquered by the British armies and fleets, the colonial forces were of the greatest assistance.

Pitt's strategy comprehended every form of pressure upon the enemy. The object which he set himself from the first was to conquer the French colonies in America, and upon this object he concentrated his main efforts. At the darkest moment of the war, in 1757, he was even willing to purchase the aid of Spain at the price of Gibraltar. Regardless of his past criticisms of continental warfare he decided to repudiate the convention of Closter-Seven and to support Frederick with men and subsidies. By the end of the war England was maintaining 70,000 men in Germany, and Frederick sent one of his ablest generals, Ferdinand of Brunswick, to be their commander. Not only did this army serve to protect Hanover and to cover Frederick's flank, but it led the French to exhaust themselves in the continental struggle. America, said Pitt, was conquered in Germany.

Pitt was, of course, prepared to take full advantage of English naval superiority. One fleet watched the French Atlantic naval bases, another was stationed near Gibraltar to keep the Toulon fleet from escaping from the Mediterranean. Other squadrons operated in American waters to check French privateering and to coöperate in attacks on the French colonies. The Indian squadron was strengthened. By these means Pitt succeeded in preventing the French from sending reinforcements to the colonies and reduced the English losses at the hands of French privateers.

A much criticised feature of his strategy, but one which has been defended by able students of warfare, and is said to have had the approval of Frederick the Great, was a series of attacks on the French coast. Their purpose was to give the home fleet some offensive work for the sake of morale, and to force the French to keep considerable forces at home to guard against attack, thus relieving the pressure on Frederick. At least five considerable expeditions were launched against French ports or naval bases, of which only one, the capture of Belle Isle off the mouth of the Loire, gained any large measure of success. How far they accomplished the larger objects which Pitt had in view, it is difficult to say.

It was in this war also that England resorted to those forms of economic pressure which constitute such an important feature of the later struggle against Napoleon. For the first time since the Anglo-French wars began, Holland, a great carrying power, was neutral. The French thought to take advantage of this by throwing open to the Dutch the ports of their colonies for the period of the war. To meet this the English government originated the famous Rule of 1756 to the effect that she would not recognize the legality of a trade in time of war which was not permitted in time of peace. The English also freely captured enemy goods on neutral vessels, and it is said that they even declared a paper blockade of all the ports of France.

It does not appear that Pitt was the originator of these measures, but he enforced them vigorously, laboring to prevent French trade from being carried on by the Dutch and Danes in the north, and by the lesser Italian states in the Mediterranean. This policy inevitably resulted in friction with the neutral powers, especially with Holland and Spain, and it was a factor, though not the most important one, in the later decision of Spain to enter the war. The attitude of the neutral powers in the War of the American Revolution is also directly traceable to their resentment at the high-handed way in which England, during this war, used her control of the sea.

The effect of these comprehensive measures was soon felt. The continental war ebbed and flowed. From the standpoint of Pitt's grand strategy it was only a vast containing operation, and so long as the French kept their forces locked up in Germany Pitt was content. It was in America that he sought and gained the decision. There the year 1758 marked the turning point. It is true that Montcalm won a last success by inflicting a severe defeat upon a greatly superior British force which tried to storm Ticonderoga, but Louisbourg was taken, and the way was open to Quebec. Fort Frontenac also, at the outlet of Lake Ontario, passed into the hands of the English, thus making it difficult for the French to send reinforcements to their western forts. One of the first fruits of this success was the abandonment of Fort Duquesne, which the English, upon occupying it, appropriately renamed Fort Pitt.

The year 1759 is known as the *annus mirabilis* because of the extraordinary number of victories won by British arms. Greatest and most spectacular of these was the capture of Quebec by Wolfe and Saunders, which broke French power in America. In the following year Montreal surrendered, and with it all Canada passed into the hands of the English. In Europe Ferdinand of Brunswick won a striking success over the French at Minden. In the West Indies the important island of Guadeloupe was taken; in West Africa, Gorée. It was in this same year that the French fleet finally abandoned East Indian waters, leaving the French force in India to its fate.

Of greater importance for the outcome of the war was the virtual destruction of the French navy at the battles of Lagos and Quiberon Bay. In the interval between the third and fourth wars the French government had devoted considerable attention to the navy, with the result that at the outset of the war, though inferior in size to the British, it was a fairly effective force. In the early years of the war the navy had assisted in the taking of Minorca, had foiled an English attack upon Louisbourg in 1757, and had been able to convoy reinforcements to India and America.

The decisive actions of the year 1759 were due to the policy adopted by the new French Minister of Foreign Affairs, the Duc de Choiseul. Choiseul felt that France had devoted too much of her energies to the continent, and determined to strike at England. The only feasible method was an invasion, for which he hoped to secure the assistance of Russia and Sweden. To have any prospect of success it was necessary to unite the two main fleets, based respectively upon Toulon and Brest. The Toulon fleet escaped into the Atlantic, but was overtaken and dispersed with the loss of several vessels by Boscawen in the battle of Lagos. This was in August. Three months later the Brest fleet put to sea, hoping still to make a descent upon the English coast, but it was pursued by Hawke into the shallow waters of Quiberon Bay and destroyed as a fighting force.

The effect of these victories was soon seen in the conquest of most of the remainder of France's colonial empire. By the end of the war there remained to her practically nothing except Haiti and the vast but thinly populated province of Louisiana. With her colonies gone and her commerce driven from the sea, France must have made peace sooner, but for the prospect, which now opened, of drawing Spain into the war.

Before considering the concluding phases of the war, it is necessary to describe the English victories in India, for it was at this time that the English laid the foundations of their Indian empire. When the war broke out, the position of the French in India was still fully as strong as that of the English. The latter had established their candidate in the Carnatic, but the French still enjoyed the friendship of the Nizam of Hyderabad, who was assiduously courted by the skilful Bussy. The French government decided, at the outbreak of the war, to send a force to India to dispute that country with the English, but so far was it from believing in the efficacy of Dupleix's policy, that the new governor-general, Count Lally, was ordered not to involve himself in native politics. Owing to various delays this force did not arrive in southern India until the spring of 1758.

Meantime important events had been occurring in another quarter of India. In 1756 the last strong native ruler of the great province of Bengal died, and was succeeded by an incapable grandson known as Siraj-ud-daula. Jealous of the growing wealth of the English settlement at Calcutta and determined to assert his authority, the new Nawab suddenly attacked and captured Calcutta in June, 1756. A small force under Clive and Admiral Watson was at once sent from Madras to recover Calcutta and quickly accomplished its object. Clive followed up this success by taking the neighboring French factory of Chandernagore, fearing an alliance between the French and Siraj-ud-daula, with whom he had made peace, but whom he by no means trusted.

Clive now listened to an intrigue on the part of some of the Nawab's officers to dethrone him and put in his place a brother-in-law of the late Nawab, Mir Jafar by name, who promised the English extensive privileges in return for their support. His only excuse was that Siraj-ud-daula had been intriguing with the French, but Clive was never a man to be deterred by scruples. Having completed his arrangements with Mir Jafar, who also commanded part of the Nawab's army, he advanced up the Ganges supported by the lighter vessels of the fleet. At Plassey, on June 23, 1757, Clive, with 3,000 men, of whom only 900 were Europeans, encountered the Nawab's army of 50,000, and largely owing to the disloyalty of Mir Jafar won a great victory. At a cost of some 23 men killed and 49 wounded the English became virtual masters of Bengal. Mir Jafar was made Nawab, but the real ruler was Clive. Control of the resources of the wealthiest and most populous of the provinces of India counted heavily in the approaching contest with the French.

In April, 1758, the French force under Lally reached India. Lally was a hot-headed man of Irish extraction, who speedily weakened his position by quarrelling with those who had most experience in Indian politics, notably Bussy. Nevertheless, he was a capable commander and made a good beginning by taking Fort St. David and besieging Madras. Here he was foiled by the ability of the English to throw in supplies, and when the French fleet, late in the summer of 1759, abandoned Indian waters Lally was left to his fate. Beaten by Eyre Coote at Wandewash in January, 1760, he was forced to surrender Pondicherry a year later to the English. By the peace of Paris the French regained the factories which they had possessed on January 1, 1749, but were compelled to limit their military forces. Henceforth, though in the later wars they entertained various schemes for driving out the English, the French ceased to count as an important factor in the affairs of India.

Probably no war so well illustrates the importance of the dynastic factor in the wars of early modern times as the Seven Years' War. It was, in fact, a series of royal deaths and successions which determined the character of the closing years of this war and had not a little to do with its outcome. The first of these was the death of Ferdinand VI, the pacific King of Spain. His successor and half-brother, Charles III, the ablest of the Spanish Bourbons, had no love for the English, and it was with the hope that he would come to the aid of France that Choiseul had undertaken his attack upon England in 1759. The unfortunate results of that attack, and the unpreparedness of Spain, justly gave Charles III pause, but his irritation against England continued unabated, and he began to press for a redress of certain grievances, seeking to link the Spanish claims with the negotiations which Choiseul was conducting for the conclusion of peace, for he desired French support in his efforts to reach a settlement with England.

Meantime, in England, another royal death had undermined the position of Pitt. Pitt had at length gained the confidence of George II, but George III, who succeeded his grandfather in 1760, was determined to be no figurehead, and through his favorite Bute was exercising more and more influence over the course of affairs. The entrance of Bute into the Cabinet was the more unfortunate for Pitt because his colleagues had long chafed under his dictatorial ways, and Newcastle in particular was unreconciled to the loss of supreme power.

To these personal differences there was added a real

difference in policy. Pitt would be satisfied with no
peace which did not completely destroy the power of
France as a commercial and maritime power. He
was especially desirous of excluding France from the
Newfoundland fisheries, which, apart from their
economic value, were regarded as a great nursery of
seamen who were indispensable in the manning of a
fleet. He also intended to keep all his colonial conquests. His principal colleagues, Newcastle and Bed-
ford, were by no means in favor of such a peace. The
latter, in particular, argued that so sweeping a victory
would upset the maritime balance of power and would
tend to produce a general combination of powers
against England. Bute was less interested in the
specific terms of peace than in securing a speedy and
satisfactory settlement, which would enable George III
to proceed with his plans of strengthening the royal
power. Since, however, the terms desired by Pitt
tended to delay a settlement, he was disposed to throw
his influence on the side of Pitt's opponents.

The crisis came in the summer of 1761. Choiseul
was anxious for peace, and would have come to terms
had Pitt shown a conciliatory disposition. The harsh
terms demanded by Pitt, however, drove him to conclude an alliance with Spain, known as the Third
Family Compact. This included a military and commercial convention and had a secret clause pledging
Spain to enter the war if by May 1, 1762, England had
not made peace. Choiseul at once took a higher tone,
and Pitt, suspecting that he had made an agreement
with Spain, prepared to break off negotiations and
advocated an immediate attack upon Spain. In the
latter demand Pitt stood almost alone in the Cabinet,
and on that issue he chose to resign (October 5, 1761).

Despite the resignation of Pitt the English government soon decided to declare war upon Spain, with the result that that power also felt the force of England's maritime supremacy. The loss of Havana and Manila was enough to convince Spain also that no profit was to be gained in a war with a nation so flushed with victory. The entrance of Spain merely served to delay the conclusion of peace and to make necessary certain changes in the peace settlement.

The determination of the English government to make peace raised also the question of its relations with Frederick the Great. Year after year Frederick had fought on, but he was almost exhausted, and even Pitt had urged him to make concessions as the price of peace. Bute and Newcastle, however, were determined to put pressure upon him by threatening to conclude a separate peace, and after the entrance of Spain they even made some approaches to Austria. At this moment Frederick was saved from almost certain destruction by the third important royal death of this period, that of the Czarina Elizabeth. Her successor, Peter III, was a great admirer of Frederick, and reversed the position of Russia by concluding an alliance with Prussia. Peter was, however, speedily overthrown, and his successor, Catherine II, determined that Russia should withdraw from the war. Despite this change in Frederick's fortunes Bute proceeded with his separate negotiations for peace and suspended the payment of subsidies to Prussia. Bute's conduct towards Frederick has been, and can be, defended, but his management of the affair was so maladroit as to produce in Frederick the ineradicable conviction that he had been deserted. Thus Bute alienated the only friend which England had and left her isolated in the hour of her triumph.

Such being the state of affairs, a settlement was soon

arranged between England and the Bourbon powers on the one hand, and between Prussia and Austria on the other. As regards the continental settlement, not an acre of territory exchanged hands. The coalition against Prussia had failed. It was England which reaped the greatest harvest from the war. In America France ceded to England Canada and the whole territory east of the Mississippi, together with several West India islands. To recover Havana, Spain yielded Florida. France, to indemnify Spain for her losses, ceded to Spain Louisiana. Thus France lost her position on the North American continent. England also recovered Minorca and gained Senegal in Africa. The practical demilitarization of the French settlements in India has already been alluded to. It is the consensus of opinion that these gains, great as they were, were not commensurate with the complete victory which England had gained. Nevertheless, they gave England such a maritime and commercial supremacy as no power hitherto had enjoyed.

The treaty was of course bitterly assailed by Pitt, and it is still criticized by those who believe that such a peace as he would have dictated would not only have crippled France permanently, but would have given England a considerable share of the commerce of the Spanish American colonies. In returning to France her chief West India colonies, it is said, the English government permitted her to retain a large share of her colonial trade, and in permitting the French to fish on the coast of Newfoundland it restored to the French their chief nursery of seamen. France therefore was not crippled as a commercial competitor, and was able to build up her naval power with unusual rapidity. Such questions must ever be matters of opinion. Even though it be granted that the unexpectedly rapid re-

covery of France had an important effect upon the
outcome of the American Revolution, it is difficult to
see how it affected either the Industrial Revolution or
the French Revolution, both of which had an enormous
influence upon the international situation. The victory
of England would, in any case, have been too complete
to save her from incurring the continued jealousy of
all her maritime rivals. The time had come when
the principle of the balance of power, which England
had done so much to develop and maintain, was to be
turned against her, when England, like France under
Louis XIV, was to stand alone against Europe.

CHAPTER III

THE MAINTENANCE OF ENGLISH MARITIME SUPREMACY

The peace of 1763 contained within itself the seeds of another war. By the completeness of her victory and the use she had made of her maritime supremacy England had aroused the jealousy of the powers, and was without a friend in Europe. In the words of Choiseul, she had destroyed the maritime balance of power. France had suffered not only defeat but humiliation, and her statesmen could not rest until they had restored her damaged prestige and had gained revenge. An earlier generation of French statesmen would have sought to raise the position of France by a vigorous continental policy; such had been the method of Fleury. The victory of England, however, seemed to prove the mercantilistic thesis that national power depended upon national wealth, and that wealth flowed principally from commerce. England, so the French argued, was intrinsically a second or third rate power. Strip her of the wealth derived from her commerce with Asia and America, and she would resume her rightful station among the nations; thus she would become a negligible factor in the affairs of Europe.

It followed that the true path to the restoration of French greatness lay in restoring French commerce, and in lessening the commercial predominance of England. The chief exponent of this idea was Choiseul, who continued to direct French foreign policy until 1770. "The true balance of power," he wrote in 1759, "resides in commerce and in America," and again: "France, in the actual posture of affairs cannot be regarded as a commercial power, which is to say that she cannot be regarded as a power of the first order." Filled with these ideas Choiseul devoted himself to the revival of French commerce, and to preparations for a war of revenge. Above all he labored to strengthen the navy, for the continued isolation of England gave him hope that the next war would be purely maritime, that England would not be able to find continental allies.

In 1770 Choiseul believed that his hour had come. Spain, which was still closely united to France by the Family Compact, fell into a dispute with England over the possession of the Falkland Islands in the Southern Atlantic. Choiseul was eager to use this dispute to precipitate a war between England and the Bourbon powers, but at this juncture, Louis XV, sceptical of the prospects of a Bourbon triumph, deprived Choiseul of his office. Thus for the time being war was postponed.

But it was not upon such chance conflicts that French statesmen counted to give them their opportunity; rather it was upon the revolt of England's American colonies. It was confidently asserted that the expulsion of the French from Canada had removed the chief reason for the continued connection between the colonies and the mother country; that having reached maturity they would inevitably, like ripe fruit, fall from the parent stem. Though many have accepted the American Revolution as sufficient proof of the correctness of this theory, to others it appears that but for stupid mismanagement on the part of British statesmen the connection between England

and her American colonies would have been indefinitely maintained, and that therefore France might have waited long for the chance of revenge.

Of the stupidity of English statesmen of this period in dealing with the American colonies there can be no doubt. At few times in her history has England been so badly governed as from 1763 to 1783. The Whig party, which had ruled the country since 1714, was now divided into cliques and factions, often divergent in policy, always quarrelling over the spoils of office. The young king, George III, bent upon making the royal power again an important factor in English affairs, shrewdly used the feuds of his opponents to ruin them. In the midst of this struggle for power the necessity of treating the two million English subjects in America with every consideration was forgotten. Penny-wise, pound-foolish politicians, disturbed by the restiveness of their constituents under the weight of taxation, decided to relieve the British taxpayer by throwing some of the burdens of empire upon the colonies. The revenue to be derived from such a policy was negligible; the risks of rebellion, had they but known it, great; war with France, once the colonies revolted, was a certainty, and England stood isolated in the midst of a hostile Europe.

Choiseul had viewed with great satisfaction the increasing friction between England and her colonies, and had sent secret agents to America to observe its progress. When friction finally kindled into revolt, a new king and a new set of ministers ruled in France. To Louis XV had succeeded, in 1774, his grandson, Louis XVI, better intentioned than his grandfather, but perhaps less able. Two paths lay before him, to pursue an ambitious foreign policy at the risk of national bankruptcy, or to follow a policy of peace,

retrenchment, and reform. For a short time the young
king listened to his reform minister Turgot, but the
beginning of the American revolt made the pursuit of
such a policy increasingly difficult. In Vergennes, the
new Minister of Foreign Affairs, Choiseul had a disciple who was determined to carry out his policy of a
war of revenge. Economy and reform had few sup-
porters among the influential classes, war and glory
were in the line of national tradition, and in May,
1776, Turgot was dismissed.

From the outset the cause of the colonies aroused
the sympathy of France. Military adventurers and
sincere friends of freedom, like Lafayette, hastened
to offer their personal services. To provide the Americans with much needed military stores, the French and
Spanish governments subsidized a pseudo-commercial
company headed by the dramatist Beaumarchais, an
ardent friend of America. Vergennes only awaited a
favorable moment, and the assurance that Spain would
assist France, to throw off the mask and join the colonies openly. But hardly had the Declaration of Independence given him assurance that the colonies had
gone too far to turn back, when news of British successes in the campaign of 1776 gave him pause. Unless
the Americans had some prospect of success he had
no desire to get embroiled in a war with England.

For over a year Vergennes maintained an attitude
of watchful waiting, while the American agents in
France, now headed by the universally popular Franklin, plied him with appeals and offers. Vergennes was
torn with conflicting emotions. Had he not already
gone too far to draw back? Might not England stamp
out the revolt, or patch up a peace with the colonies,
and then turn her forces in America against the French
West Indies? All doubts were finally resolved by the

surrender of Burgoyne at Saratoga (October, 1777). No sooner had the news reached Paris than Vergennes sent a confidential agent to Franklin to negotiate a treaty of alliance. Even when Spain refused to join him, he persisted, and on February 6, 1778, the treaty was signed. War with England was now inevitable.

It is to be noted that the French government expressly disavowed any intention of attempting to recover Canada. In fact, Vergennes preferred to see it continue in British hands as a pledge of the continued dependence of the United States upon France. What France chiefly sought to accomplish was to weaken England by tearing from her control her most populous colonies, and to establish in America a political and commercial satellite of France. France would profit from the trade of America, would regain some of the influence in America which she had lost in the preceding war, and would get revenge. In short, it was Vergennes and not Canning who initiated the policy of calling a new world into existence to redress the balance of the old.

The war of 1778-1783 was unlike any other Anglo-French war. For once there were no continental complications; the conflict was purely maritime and colonial. Furthermore, the universal dislike of England made it possible for Vergennes to build up a coalition of maritime powers against her. To secure the aid of Spain proved more difficult than Vergennes anticipated, for the Spaniards were caught in a dilemma. They hated England, but because of their own extensive colonial empire, they feared to aid a colonial revolt. Finally, in 1779, at the price of promises of French assistance in the recovery of Gibraltar, Florida, Minorca, and Honduras, they agreed to join in the war. This purely self-seeking attitude on the part of the

Spanish made their assistance during the war of little value, and, as will shortly appear, greatly increased the difficulty of making a satisfactory peace.

Of the other maritime powers, Holland was forced into the war by the English in 1780, on the ground that it was better to be at war with the Dutch than to permit them, under the cover of neutrality, to aid England's enemies. The other maritime powers showed their hostility by joining the so-called Armed Neutrality of the North, established in the spring of 1780 by Catherine of Russia with French encouragement. As a protest against the rules of maritime war enforced by England in this and the preceding war, this league asserted the most liberal principles concerning contraband, blockade, and the rights of neutrals. To enforce their declaration the northern powers commissioned a large fleet of war vessels, and England was compelled to modify her treatment of neutral powers. Moreover, the refusal of Russia to consider naval stores contraband of war made it impossible for the English to prevent France from securing such stores from the Baltic. To borrow the expressive phrase of a recent historian, Great Britain stood alone against the trading world.

That England, confronted by such odds, escaped a worse disaster proves that her maritime power was far more solidly based than Choiseul had believed. Nor was her escape due to the efficiency of her government. At this crisis no Marlborough or Pitt directed English policy and strategy. The nominal head of the government was Lord North, good-natured, loyal to the king, of mediocre talents. The real ruler of England was George III, whose chief asset was a kind of stubborn persistence. When France broke with England the nation clamored for Pitt, now Earl of Chatham, but the king refused to permit him to take office except as a subordinate of North. It mattered little, for within a few weeks death had removed the one Englishman who might have saved the Empire. That even he could have saved it is by no means certain.

English military operations were handicapped by the incompetence, and worse, of North's colleagues. At the head of the Admiralty was the corrupt and debauched Sandwich, who by graft and favoritism had greatly decreased the efficiency of that branch of the service. Some of the ablest admirals were Whigs, who could scarce bring themselves to serve, even against the ancient enemy, under one in whom they had so little confidence. The ships were in poor repair, the dockyards neglected, the supply of naval stores for building new ships and repairing old, dangerously low.

The military operations in America were directed from England by Lord George Germain. More honest and efficient than Sandwich, he had the grave fault of giving too minute orders to the commanders in America, orders which his lack of acquaintance with that country often made inappropriate. The higher officers in America lacked ability, or enthusiasm for the war, sometimes both. As it was difficult to get Englishmen to enlist for the American war, the ministry was forced to hire German troops (Hessians) to subdue the colonies, soldiers whose military services were scarcely commensurate with the hatred which their coming aroused in America against the government which sent them.

It is probable that the strategy of both the combatants was defective. France had such a chance as she had not had since 1692 to cripple the English navy, perhaps even to invade England and compel her to come to terms. The French fleet was somewhat smaller than the English, but was in much better condition to fight. So unprepared were the English that in the spring of 1778 the French were able to get to sea a much larger squadron, but as they did not contemplate an attack upon England except in alliance with Spain, the chance for that year was lost. In 1779 the Franco-Spanish fleet outnumbered the English Channel fleet three to two, but its efforts to clear the Channel for an invasion of England failed miserably. Thenceforth the Bourbon allies concentrated their efforts upon their individual objectives, the Spanish upon Gibraltar, the French upon operations in the West Indies and American waters.

The English might possibly have offset Bourbon naval superiority by blockading the French and Spanish naval bases, as Pitt had done, but this they neglected to do. Consequently French and Spanish squadrons operated freely both in European and American waters, and all the English attempted to do was to prevent the capture of Gibraltar, and to maintain a squadron equal to that of the French in American waters. Thus the naval operations of the war were diffused, and neither side established anywhere a clear naval superiority. In Europe the English saved Gibraltar and preserved England from attack, but in the West Indies the French had the better of the argument, so that by the close of 1781 of all her West India possessions England retained only Jamaica, Barbados, and Antigua.

The ability to operate freely in all waters gave the French a chance also to challenge the British in India. Their opportunity came from the restiveness of the native powers at the growth of British ascendency. Bengal was quiet under the firm rule of Warren Hastings, but in the south of India there had arisen in the state of Mysore an ambitious military adventurer by the name of Hyder Ali. This remarkable man not only aroused the principal native states of south India against the British, but appealed for aid from the French at Mauritius. Thereupon the French government sent a considerable fleet to Indian waters under Suffren, one of the ablest of their commanders. Within little more than a year Suffren fought no less than five engagements with the English fleet, in which he maintained a slight advantage, but as in the days of Dupleix French reliance upon the native powers proved futile, Hyder Ali was beaten, and British ascendency in India remained intact.

The war soon resolved itself into a contest of endurance. It has been generally assumed that the defeat of England was inevitable, but such was perhaps not the case, even though many English statesmen, including Lord North himself, felt that the case was hopeless. England's financial resources gave her an enormous advantage over poverty-stricken America and bankrupt France, and her naval position improved as the war continued. It was with difficulty that Vergennes, in 1780, persuaded Louis XVI to fight on for another year, and early in 1781 Austria and Russia offered mediation. Had the campaign of 1781 not proved decisive the probable outcome would have been an inconclusive peace.

The great stake of the war was the fate of America and it was there that the ultimate decision must be gained. The French had not originally intended to send troops to America, believing that with some assistance in money and munitions, and the coöperation of the French fleet, the Americans would be able to establish their independence. As the war continued, however, the American efforts grew feebler and feebler. Bankruptcy overtook the loosely organized Confederation, the British overran large sections of the South, and even Washington was on the verge of despair. In 1780 the French government, acting on the advice of Lafayette, sent over a force of six thousand men under Rochambeau, which, for nearly a year, remained inactive at Newport. At the close of 1780 so desperate was the situation that the Americans sent a special appeal to France for immediate financial and military assistance. Their request was granted, and the result was the campaign of Yorktown.

There were at this time two considerable British armies in America, one under Clinton at New York, and one under Cornwallis in the South. It was decided by Washington and Rochambeau to strike a blow at the latter as soon as news arrived that the French fleet was on its way from the West Indies. How Washington and Rochambeau cleverly slipped past Clinton, how the French fleet convoyed them across Chesapeake Bay, how the French and Americans trapped Cornwallis at Yorktown, how the victory of De Grasse off the Capes of the Chesapeake prevented the British from sending Cornwallis reinforcements, and how Cornwallis surrendered on October 19, 1781, is a story too well known to need retelling. The victory was decisive. Almost alone George III wished to continue the war, but he now lost control of the situation, the North ministry resigned, and the Whig government which took its place at once began negotiations for peace.

The peace negotiations at Paris revealed a bewildering conflict of interests. The English Whig ministry sought to reconcile the Americans by granting them favorable terms of peace, and to weaken, or disrupt, the Franco-American alliance. The Americans were pledged not to make a separate peace, and though friendly enough with France were on the worst possible terms with Spain. Vergennes had the almost impossible task of satisfying both Spain and the Americans. Although the fighting in America was practically over, the negotiations were considerably influenced by military operations elsewhere during the year 1782. In the West Indies the Bourbon powers received a severe setback at the hands of Admiral Rodney, who in April of that year won a smashing victory over a French fleet which had intended to attack Jamaica. In European waters the English lost Minorca, but defeated the final Spanish attempt to take Gibraltar. This last event in particular made it difficult for Vergennes to satisfy his Spanish allies.

In the final analysis it was the action of the Americans which proved the determining factor. Evidence came to the American commissioners which seemed to prove that Vergennes was prepared to sacrifice American interests in the Mississippi valley and the Newfoundland fisheries to please Spain. This would have been no violation of the letter of the treaty of alliance, which did not cover these points, and Franklin still trusted Vergennes. He was outvoted, however, by his colleagues, Jay and John Adams, with the result that the English and Americans came to an agreement in November, 1782. The Americans had not consulted Vergennes in making terms, but safeguarded themselves against the charge of breaking faith by arranging that the Anglo-American agreement should not take effect except as part of a general peace. The concessions which they secured from the English, however, made the task of Vergennes still more difficult, and it was with great reluctance that Spain accepted Florida,

Minorca, and a definition of British rights in Honduras in place of Gibraltar, which had been her principal objective.

For France Vergennes demanded little, the cession of Senegal, complete possession of St. Pierre and Miquelon, the right to fortify Dunkirk. Not for such things had he fought, but to disrupt the British Empire, to humiliate a rival, to restore French prestige. All this he had accomplished, and, as he fondly believed, much more, for it was the general opinion that the decline of England as a maritime power would follow inevitably upon the loss of her American colonies. At the very least the maritime balance of power had been restored, and if the predictions of English decline were fulfilled, the war would mark an epoch in the maritime rivalry of England and France.

These predictions, as we now realize, were based upon an inadequate comprehension of the situation. In reality England's strength was not seriously impaired by her defeat. Financially she was better off than her rival. Her naval power was intact; it was in the last year of the war that her fleets had won their greatest victories. Her supremacy in India was undisturbed. Her position in the West Indies, where more than a quarter of her overseas trade originated, was not seriously weakened. The loss of the continental colonies, damaging as it was to England's prestige, did not result in the economic loss predicted by the mercantilists. It was discovered by Hamilton, during Washington's first administration, that seven-eighths of America's trade was still with England. The economic bonds which had bound America to England thus proved far stronger and more enduring than the political. In Europe also, though England remained isolated, no vital interest had been injured, for the con-

tinental balance was undisturbed, and the Franco-
Austrian alliance was a guarantee against French
aggression in the Low Countries.

Meantime, both on the continent and in questions of
commerce and colonies, new forces were at work which
tended to improve the relations of England and France.
The rapid advance of Russia in eastern Europe, and
the continued decline of Poland and Turkey, were disturbing to both.   France was threatened with a loss
of influence in that quarter, while England began to
realize that Russia was rapidly becoming a more dangerous threat than France to English interests in India
and the Levant.   Shelburne, who for a brief period
headed the English ministry, was convinced that the
advance of Russia made advisable a reconciliation
with France.   "Let us unite and we shall give the law
to Europe," he is reported to have remarked during
the course of the peace negotiations of 1782-83.   Thus
appeared on the horizon a new source of interest for
England in continental affairs, one which, known in
the nineteenth century as the Eastern Question, ab-
sorbed more and more of her attention, and one in
which the interests of England and France tended as
often to be similar as to be discordant.

As regards commerce and colonies the new school of
laissez-faire economists was already impressing its
opinions upon statesmen.   Turgot had held office for a
short time in France; in England men like Shelburne,
Burke, and the younger Pitt showed some sympathy
with their ideas, and were familiar with the classic
work of this school, Adam Smith's *Wealth of Nations*.
If, as these economists argued, commerce and industry
flourished best when governments most let them alone,
and if colonies, as soon as they reached maturity, were
inevitably to separate from the mother country, what

was the good of prohibitive tariffs and of the fierce rivalry for colonies which had characterized the last two centuries of European history? These ideas were reinforced in England by more practical considerations. There the Industrial Revolution was already under way, and the growing ability of English manufacturers to undersell foreign competitors made them less and less fearful of foreign competition, consequently more and more willing to lower English tariffs in order to get reciprocal concessions from foreign countries.

The Anglo-French commercial treaty of 1786 was a practical illustration of the growing influence in both countries of these more liberal ideas. For the first time in over a century English and French statesmen were willing to admit that the two countries could trade with one another to mutual advantage. The objects of the treaty were political as well as commercial, for, as one of the French negotiators said, it was intended to diminish "the national hatred, which has hitherto separated France from England."

The continued isolation of England, and the further extension of French influence on the continent, still aroused English fear and jealousy, but when France lost Vergennes, by some regarded as the ablest French Foreign Minister of the century, and when in 1788 the younger Pitt succeeded in negotiating a triple alliance with Prussia and Holland, even this root of bitterness was removed. A dispassionate observer of the state of Europe in 1788 might well have predicted a long period of peace like that which followed the peace of Utrecht.

Such was the situation when the French Revolution burst upon Europe, blotting out the old landmarks and totally deranging the system of international relations. Its first results were inevitably damaging to the posi-

tion of France and favorable to that of England.
While France was plunged into anarchy and threatened
with foreign invasion, England remained at peace, and
prospered exceedingly under the skilful rule of the
younger Pitt. By refusing in 1790 to support Spain
against England in a dispute concerning the right of
the English to trade and settle on the northwest coast of
North America, the so-called Nootka Sound affair,
France virtually terminated the Bourbon Family Compact which for two generations had been a disturbing
factor in Anglo-French relations. However perturbed
continental monarchs might feel at the substitution in
France of a limited monarchy for the old Divine Right
absolutism, in England the first phases of the Revolution were regarded as a flattering attempt to imitate
the British Constitution, and as the best possible guarantee of the continuance of peace. Even the gloomy
prophecies of Burke's famous *Reflections on the French
Revolution* (1790) failed to arouse his countrymen, or
to affect the policy of the ministry, which was one of
strict non-intervention.

It turned out, however, that Burke had more accu-
rately assessed the tremendous forces liberated by the
Revolution than most of his countrymen. Its progress
could not be halted at the point where it met the approval of Englishmen, or where it threatened no English interest. In August, 1792, Louis XVI was made
a prisoner, in September France was proclaimed a Republic, and in the following January the French king
died on the scaffold. At the same time the French
armies, hitherto on the defensive, drove out the invad-
ing Austro-Prussian forces and began to overflow the
boundaries of France all along the eastern border. As
late as the first week of November, 1792, the British

government still contemplated no change of policy. Thereafter relations with France grew rapidly worse, and on February 1, 1793, the French Republic declared war. Thus with startling suddenness the hope of a prolonged peace was snatched away, and the two nations began that desperate conflict which lasted with one brief intermission until the battle of Waterloo.

It has seemed to many writers that England might have avoided war in 1793, and various reasons have been assigned for the failure of the government to do so. Pitt's Whig opponents charged him with joining the absolute monarchs of the continent in a crusade to restore the French monarchy, and in truth the execution of Louis XVI aroused such a feeling of horror in England that many Englishmen were powerfully influenced by this motive. It has also been charged that Pitt entered upon this war to complete the work of his father, to destroy France as a commercial and colonial rival. The consensus of opinion, however, is that this was not an anti-revolutionary crusade, nor yet a contest for maritime supremacy, but a war to preserve the balance of power. When the French armies in the autumn of 1792 overran Belgium and threatened Holland, at that time England's ally, when the French government tore up the ancient treaties closing the river Scheldt, when it issued decrees which were justly interpreted as an incitement to the peoples of Europe to refashion their institutions according to the principles of the Revolution, and which appeared to commit the French Republic to a crusade against the monarchies of Europe, the balance of power was threatened. The response of the people of the lands bordering upon France to these decrees opened the way for an indefinite extension of French influence, if not of French political power. As re-

gards the Low Countries, at least, such an extension of
French influence ran counter to one of the fundamental principles of British policy.

The utterances of British statesmen reinforce this
verdict. "This government," wrote Pitt's Foreign
Secretary, Lord Grenville, "adhering to maxims which
it has followed for more than a century, will never see
with indifference, that France shall make herself, either
directly or indirectly, sovereign of the Low Countries,
or general arbiters of the rights and liberties of
Europe." More simply still did Pitt define the issue
when challenged by his opponents in Parliament. It
was a question, he said, of England's security, which
was endangered by the aggressions of revolutionary
France, and he was willing at any time to sign a peace
which would guarantee that security. To quote Pitt's
biographer Rose, "National security was wholly incom-
patible with the possession of Holland, or even the Bel-
gic Provinces, by France."

The war began under conditions which seemed to
insure a speedy overthrow of the French Republic.
The newly established French government was torn by
factional strife, large sections of the south and west of
France were in revolt, the army was an uncertain
quantity, the navy was disorganized, the finances were
totally deranged. Furthermore, France was at war
with Austria, Prussia, Sardinia, Holland, and Spain, as
well as with England. Had this been a war of the old
sort, France must shortly have succumbed to her enemies. Her position in 1793 was far more desperate
than it had been in 1709 or in 1760.

Unfortunately for the peace of Europe this was not a
war of the old sort. For almost the first time in European history, the driving force was supplied not by the
governments, but by the peoples. The attack of mon-

archical Europe upon the French Republic did more
than anything else to reconcile the French people to the
ruthless stamping out of internal dissent and to the
establishment of a dictatorship. It was the people of
France who crowded into the French armies, fired with
a zeal not only to defend the soil of the Fatherland, but
to spread the blessings of liberty, equality, and frater-
nity among neighboring peoples. It was because these
neighboring peoples also embraced with fervor the principles of the Revolution that the French armies found
everywhere, when they crossed the French frontier,
friends and not enemies. The statesmen of Europe
were confronted by a force which they could neither
measure nor comprehend; they understood only the old
order of things which was rapidly passing away.

No statesman failed more completely to comprehend
these new forces than the younger Pitt. Essentially a
financier and economist of the type of Walpole or Glad-
stone, he was unfitted by temperament and training to
be a great war minister. He lacked the dæmonic
energy of his father, and his policy was not illumined
by those lightning-like flashes of insight which were
characteristic of that statesman. He could hearten men
to bear the intolerable, he could not inspire them to do
the impossible. He was a traditionalist, not an inno-
vator. He relied, says his biographer, "on the statics
of statecraft rather than on the dynamics of nation-
ality." He is best described in the phrase of his
disciple Canning as "the pilot who weathered the
storm." Confronted by a disturbance of cyclonic force,
he was no miracle-worker to bid the storm cease and
the waves be still. His was the less spectacular, and
no less necessary, task of guiding the ship of state
safely through.

The war policy of Pitt has been severely criticized by

Macaulay and others. It has been said that he should have made the war frankly an anti-revolutionary crusade, that by so doing he could have aroused in England something of the same fervor which animated France, that he could then have created great armies and despatched them to the continent, where in concert with the continental powers and the French Royalists they might have reproduced the victories of Marlborough in Flanders, the triumphs of the Black Prince on the soil of France.

In judging the validity of these criticisms the time element must be considered. It was at the beginning of the war, if ever, that there was a good chance of destroying the French revolutionary government and of bringing France quickly to terms. It was in 1793 that the French Royalist resistance in the south and west of France was at its height; the French armies were not yet effectively organized and commanded. But at no time have the British been able to despatch large forces to the continent at the beginning of a war; they have always been forced to rely mainly on their continental allies.

What happened in the campaigns of 1793-94 is instructive. In 1793 Pitt did send a considerable force to the continent, which with the assistance of the German and Dutch allies repelled the French from Holland, and drove them out of Belgium. In the same year the English and Spanish fleets with Royalist assistance occupied Toulon. But even before the end of the year the tide began to turn. The allies were checked along the eastern border, the Royalist movements were largely suppressed, Toulon was recovered, Carnot was organizing effective armies. At this point the efforts of Austria and Prussia slackened because of their anxiety over the designs of Russia upon Poland. In

1794 the French recovered Belgium, and in the early months of 1795 they overran Holland and organized it into a republic after the French model. The British forces were now withdrawn from the continent, not again to operate there in any numbers until the beginning of the Peninsular War in 1808. In 1795 also Prussia and Spain deserted the coalition, which was now reduced to England, Austria, and Sardinia, and already the French dominated Europe as far east as the Rhine. Such were the results of the first great efforts to keep revolutionary France within bounds.

Often unsuccessful in their military efforts at the beginning of a war, the British inevitably made the utmost use of their maritime supremacy. The French navy, which so recently had fought the English on equal terms, was thoroughly disorganized by the Revolution, and English control of the sea was, and remained, substantially unchallenged. Extraordinarily successful in creating armies, the successive revolutionary governments of France were unable to create an effective navy. British successes at the beginning of the war still further established their supremacy. Most of the Mediterranean squadron was captured or destroyed when the British and Spanish took Toulon; the Atlantic fleet was severely handled by Admiral Howe in the Battle of the First of June (1794).

At no time in her history did England use her maritime supremacy more ruthlessly than in this war. This was made possible by the virtual isolation of France. Of the chief maritime powers Spain and Holland were, until 1795, allied with England. Russia, which in 1780 had headed the League of Armed Neutrality, agreed to assist England in preventing neutrals from trading with France, and by her attitude not only prevented the Scandinavian countries from resisting British measures, but made it difficult for France to secure naval stores from the Baltic. The one new factor in the situation was the United States, which might have supplied France with provisions and West India products. This the British prevented by placing provisions on the list of contraband, and by a strict enforcement of the Rule of 1756. The United States was almost goaded into war, but finally decided not to risk a contest with England, and in the Jay treaty of 1795 made important concessions to the British point of view. As a result of England's efforts, by 1799 there was scarce a vessel on the ocean flying the French flag, while the overseas trade of England had doubled.

Oblivious of the fact that France was increasingly dependent upon neutrals for many things, successive French governments attempted to retaliate by copying British methods, although for the enforcement of their decrees they had to rely mainly upon privateers. The policy of attempting to prevent neutrals from trading with England, begun haltingly by the Jacobins in 1793 and continued with increasing vigor by the Directory, reached its culmination in the Continental System of Napoleon. Its effects were highly unfortunate, for it failed of its principal object, and it deprived France of the sympathy of neutrals like the United States, who, owing to the severity of the British measures, might otherwise have favored France.

What Pitt's critics have chiefly in mind, apparently, in the criticism of his conduct of the war, is his use of British forces in the West Indies rather than in Europe, "filching sugar islands," a contemporary critic called it. In judging this policy it must be borne in mind that the trade in West India products constituted at that time one of the most important branches of international commerce, and that more than a fourth of Eng-

land's overseas trade originated in this area. Furthermore, the bulk of France's remaining colonial empire
was in the Caribbean. To deprive France of the
products of her colonies, and of the power to distribute
those products over Europe, was to strike a deadly blow
at French commerce. Exhaustion alone, according to
Pitt's most eloquent defender, Admiral Mahan, suffices
to bring to terms a people which whole-heartedly sup-
ports a foreign war, and the surest way to produce exhaustion is by economic pressure; military pressure
alone seldom, or never, suffices. From the failure of
military efforts to suppress revolutionary movements
such as those of Holland, the American colonies, and
Russia the historian could certainly adduce much evidence to support such a thesis.

The English efforts to capture the French West India islands were only moderately successful, for by
extending to the slaves also the blessings of the Rights
of Man the French aroused among the blacks a revolutionary fervor which enabled them to recover Guadeloupe and St. Lucia and to stir up servile insurrections
in some of the English islands. It was this same policy
which paralyzed the English efforts in Haiti, the wealthiest of all the French colonies, and which enabled the
negroes of that island to free themselves from any
European control. In a larger sense, however, the
English were successful, for they secured a practical
monopoly of the trade in West India products, and the
inability of the continent to secure West India coffee
and sugar was an important factor in the breakdown of
Napoleon's Continental System.

It was upon a supposed common devotion to democ-
racy and the Rights of Man that the French also relied
to secure the assistance of the United States. In 1793
the Citizen Genêt was sent as minister to the American

Republic with instructions to use that country as a base of operations against the neighboring British and Spanish colonies. Multitudes of Americans were ready to assist him, but the attitude of the American government brought to nought his efforts. Washington's Neutrality Proclamation of 1793 marked an epoch in the relations of America to Europe, for it was an expression of the determination of America to repel all attempts by European statesmen to drag her into their quarrels.

With the peace of Basel (1795) the first phase of the war ended and the position of England grew rapidly worse. Holland and Spain now threw in their lot with France, and declared war upon England, thus giving the French a considerable accession of naval strength. In 1796 the English fleet was withdrawn from the Mediterranean, and the young Bonaparte was left with a free hand in Italy. Sardinia and Austria were brought to terms, the latter in 1797, and much of Italy came under French influence. For a time England stood alone against a France which dominated the continent to a far greater extent than Louis XIV had ever done.

By this time the French objective in the war had changed; no longer was it a crusade for the Rights of Man. The Directory, which came into office in 1795, began to talk of natural boundaries for France quite in the spirit of Richelieu or Louis XIV. In England, following the collapse of the first coalition, there was a strong movement for peace, and had the French government been willing to moderate its aims, peace might have been attained. The French, however, were flushed with victory and determined to bring England to terms. At this moment the growing signs of rebellion in Ireland seemed to offer them a chance to strike from that quarter, and in response to appeals for aid from

Irish emissaries a considerable force was despatched to Ireland in the autumn of 1796. It was beaten off more by a series of disastrous storms than by the efforts of the English fleet. In the following year the French pinned their hopes to a combination of the Spanish, French, and Dutch fleets to support an invasion of Ireland, but the Spanish fleet was shattered by Jervis in February at Cape St. Vincent, and the Dutch by Duncan in October at Camperdown. British naval supremacy was thus maintained.

The year 1797 was one of the darkest in England's history. The country was threatened with invasion, for a time the navy was paralyzed by an extensive mutiny, a severe financial crisis resulted in the suspension of specie payments, and Austria, England's one remaining ally, had to accept a separate peace. Serious peace negotiations were carried on in the summer of that year, and France had only to give England guarantees for her security to gain an honorable peace. Unfortunately for England, for France, and for Europe, the war party in France secured control by the coup d'état of September 4, 1797. The ruling spirits of the French government were now the subtle diplomat Talleyrand and the ambitious soldier Bonaparte. The peace negotiations with England were broken off, and France again embarked upon the dual policy which had brought disaster to Louis XIV, the policy of extending her sway over the continent and of challenging the commercial and colonial supremacy of England.

Between these two policies the French saw an intimate connection. England's maritime predominance, they believed, not only stood in the way of France's commercial development, but enabled the British to maintain the balance of power in Europe. It was England, they argued, which was always promoting strife

on the continent in order to weaken France and to en-
hance her own commercial greatness. With such a
power no peace was possible. "Our Government,"
wrote Bonaparte in 1797, "must destroy the English
monarchy, or it must expect itself to be destroyed by
these active islanders."

There were two possible methods of striking at England. The one favored hitherto was an invasion, either
directly, or through Ireland. This was rejected by
Bonaparte because the French had no reasonable hope
of controlling the sea. Long afterwards he admitted
that he let slip a great opportunity. In the spring of
1798 Ireland broke into open revolt, and it is the
general opinion that it would have been possible for the
French to throw sufficient forces into that island to
affect the outcome of the entire war. But Bonaparte's
Italian campaign had directed his thoughts towards
Egypt, which had long been an object of interest to
French policy. "The time is not far distant," he wrote,
"when we shall feel that truly to destroy England, we
must take possession of Egypt." Possession of Egypt
would serve many purposes. It might enable France to
cut off England's eastern trade, perhaps to dislodge the
English from India. It would be the beginning of a
new colonial empire for France. It might even be a
stepping stone to the destruction of the Ottoman Empire. In imagination, Bonaparte saw himself, from
Constantinople, giving the law to Europe and western
Asia.

The results of Bonaparte's Egyptian expedition
(1798) were altogether disastrous. Deprived of French
support, the Irish revolt was so thoroughly crushed
that Ireland ceased to be a possible base against England. By seizing Malta on his way to Egypt, Bonaparte
ensured the adhesion of Russia to the new coalition

which Pitt was forming, for the Czar had been elected Grand Master of the Knights of Malta. Nelson's great victory at the Battle of the Nile (August 1, 1798) left the French force stranded in Egypt, where it ultimately surrendered to the English (1801). Bonaparte himself returned to Europe in 1799 to find France beaten to her knees by the second coalition.

As another result of this Egyptian expedition must be reckoned the formal establishment of English control in India. To guard the approaches to India the English had already, after the Dutch declared against them, seized the Cape of Good Hope and Ceylon, but the French still held their naval base at Mauritius. The new threat to India implied by the invasion of Egypt was not lost upon the British. The situation was the more serious in that the native powers were increasingly resentful of the British predominance. The most active among them, Tippoo Sultan of Mysore, son of that Hyder Ali who had challenged the British at the time of the American Revolution, was known to have been intriguing with the French. Shortly after his arrival in Egypt Bonaparte despatched letters to Tippoo announcing that he was on his way to free India from the iron yoke of England.

Fortunately for the English the situation was taken in hand by one of the ablest of their Indian rulers, Richard Wellesley, brother of the more famous Duke of Wellington. Wellesley speedily isolated and crushed Tippoo, and then proceeded to attack and vanquish other native powers whose attitude had been threatening. As a result, when Wellesley was recalled in 1805, British power in India was more firmly established than ever before.

The accentuated emphasis upon the commercial and colonial phases of the war spurred the English to fresh activity in the West Indies. Though Haiti was abandoned to the blacks, all the other French islands except Guadeloupe were occupied, together with Spanish Trinidad and the Dutch possessions in Guiana and the Caribbean. Pitt also listened sympathetically to the plans of the Spanish American revolutionist, Miranda, for revolutionizing Spanish America. Miranda hoped also to secure the aid of the United States, which was at this time engaged in a quasi-war with France because of French treatment of American commerce. The Angophile party in America headed by Alexander Hamilton favored an Anglo-American attack upon Spain's American empire, but the cautious and sceptical American President, John Adams, would give no countenance to such a scheme, and Pitt was too busy in Europe to engage in so vast an enterprise.

Again was Pitt disappointed in his hopes, for the second coalition broke up even more rapidly than the first. Bonaparte's second Italian campaign (1800) brought Austria to terms, and the Czar, disgusted at the conduct of his allies, deserted them. So great was his anger that he allowed Napoleon to persuade him to revive the Armed Neutrality of the North. The danger that the Baltic would be closed, and the indispensable supply of naval stores cut off, led the British to take drastic action. A fleet was sent which crushed the Danes at Copenhagen and prevented the closing of the Baltic. The assassination of the Czar at almost the same time was the finishing blow to the Armed Neutrality. His successor, Alexander I, abandoned the League and made important concessions as regards England's maritime code. The two antagonists had come to a stalemate; France dominated the continent but England still controlled the sea.

Under the circumstances it was natural that they

should pause to take breath, but it was inevitable that a peace, so concluded, should be unsatisfactory. The terms of the peace of Amiens, concluded on the part of England by the weak Addington ministry (Pitt had resigned because of a disagreement with the king over Irish affairs), have been almost universally condemned. Says a recent critic, "While sacrificing the conquests achieved by the British overseas, it failed to assure the Balance of Power on the Continent." Of all her conquests England kept only Trinidad and Ceylon, and she exacted no guarantees against further French aggression upon the continent.

Had Napoleon, who now completely dominated French policy, been content to pursue a pacific and conciliatory policy, the peace might have lasted for a considerable period, but for a military adventurer long to pursue such a policy was impossible. Nor did Napoleon even make the attempt. His continued aggressions in Holland and Switzerland made the English vastly uneasy; his refusal to make a commercial treaty with England defeated the hopes of those who welcomed peace as a relief from the commercial conflict; his manifest efforts to reconstruct France's colonial empire by attempting to recover Haiti and Santo Domingo, by securing the cession of Louisiana from Spain, and by intrigues in Egypt, Asia Minor, and India, touched the British at their most sensitive point. The ostensible cause of the rupture, which occurred in May, 1803, was the refusal of the British to surrender Malta, the value of which for preventing French aggression in the Levant was now recognized. In reality, however, peace between England and Napoleon was an impossibility.

The war which began in the spring of 1803 was the longest and most bitterly contested of the seven conflicts making up the Second Hundred Years' War. It was a struggle for existence, in which neither side asked or gave quarter, and in which neither hesitated to use any weapon at its disposal. The first phases of the war were necessarily naval in character. England was without continental allies, and in 1804, regarding Spain as a tool of Napoleon, drove that power also into war. To bring England to terms Napoleon planned an invasion, and gathered a great army along the Channel coast. At first he considered ferrying a large force across the Channel to make a surprise attack. Abandoning this as impracticable, he ordered a concentration of the various French and Spanish squadrons, hoping to control the Channel long enough to throw his army across. To these plans Nelson's crowning triumph at Trafalgar (October 21, 1805) was a fatal blow. The idea of an invasion of England was now abandoned.

Meantime Pitt, who had resumed his place as premier, had laboriously constructed a third coalition, consisting of Austria, Russia, and Sweden, to give Napoleon occupation on the continent. The crushing of Austria at Austerlitz (December 2, 1805) was the beginning of the end of the coalition. It was also a fatal blow to Pitt, who died some seven weeks later, exhausted by his long efforts to bring within bounds the power of France. The ship was still riding out the gale, but the storm was by no means abated. In Pitt's disciples, Canning and Castlereagh, England found new pilots to take up and complete his unfinished task.

The initiative now rested with Napoleon, who for a time passed from triumph to triumph until the whole continent lay at his feet. How to bring the Island Power to terms was the problem which most puzzled him. He was still fascinated by the idea of striking at England's eastern empire, which was regarded as the principal basis of her wealth and prosperity. A more immediately practicable plan was to put in operation systematically the policy of commercial war which earlier French governments had half-heartedly pursued. To exclude British goods from the continent and to destroy as far as possible British overseas trade might prove the successful method. Hence the Continental System, which Napoleon initiated with his Berlin decree of 1806.

It was the Continental System which more than anything else caused the downfall of Napoleon. It may have come perilously near to success, as some maintain, but the difficulties of enforcing it were almost insuperable. To reduce England to exhaustion required time, and every year the system lasted the difficulties of maintaining it were increased. Even France was to some extent dependent upon British manufactures, which were smuggled in, or imported under a system of licenses. It is said that part of the Grand Army which invaded Russia in 1812 was clothed with English cloth. More damaging still was the resentment which the attempted enforcement of the system created among the subject peoples. No longer were the French regarded as liberators, but as oppressors. Deprived of English manufactures and colonial foodstuffs, the peoples of central Europe became restless under French control. The result was a nationalist reaction against the Napoleonic Empire which brought into play a force which Napoleon was powerless to combat. In the peoples of Europe who sought their freedom Pitt's successors found allies far more potent and far more dependable than the governments which had so often failed him.

To close every possible loophole for the entrance

of British goods to the continent became, after 1807, the chief object of Napoleon's policy. One such loophole was the Iberian peninsula, and it was Napoleon's intervention in Spain which produced, in 1808, the first great nationalist uprising. This it was which gave the British a chance to reorient their policy. In words reminiscent of the French decrees of 1792 Canning, speaking for the British government, now announced that England would regard as her ally any nation which would oppose the common enemy of all nations. An alliance with the Spanish patriots and the despatch to the Peninsula of a British army commanded by Sir Arthur Wellesley, better known as the Duke of Wellington, made good these words; there resulted the Peninsular War, that running sore, which Napoleon could never heal.

Curiously enough it was the Continental System which deprived Napoleon of any chance of pursuing his alternative plan of attack upon England. To purchase the adhesion of Russia to his system he was forced in 1807, at the treaty of Tilsit, to give the Czar a free hand in the east of Europe. While Napoleon sought the friendship of Turkey, Persia, and Afghanistan, the powers which guarded the land route to India, his ally the Czar picked a quarrel with Turkey which destroyed French influence not only at Constantinople but throughout the Near and Middle East. By the close of the Napoleonic wars English influence was far greater in that quarter than ever before. Here, as in India itself, the French menace merely resulted in the increase of British power.

Even in Europe the Russian alliance failed to produce the hoped-for results. Influenced by the restiveness of his people under their deprivations, the Czar abandoned the Continental System at the close of 1810. There followed the fatal march to Moscow, the rising of Germany, the War of Liberation, Elba, Waterloo. The sea power had conquered because it had put itself on the side of the peoples of Europe who refused to endure an intolerable economic system.

In the midst of this conflict the English were able also to conquer most of the French and Dutch colonies. Out of respect for their allies the English forbore to aid the Spanish and Portuguese colonies in America, which already were restive under European control, but the European war destroyed the old system of rigid commercial control, and political independence was not far distant. When the colonies did revolt, it was the action of England which was decisive. The protest of Canning at the threat of French intervention, capped by the American Monroe Doctrine (1823), ensured the downfall of Spain as a colonizing power. Thus England concluded the work of ruining her colonial rivals, either by conquering their colonies, or by enabling them to set up as independent states. Thenceforth for half a century, as there was but one first class commercial power, so there was but one important colonial power.

This belated result of the Anglo-French conflict merely put the capstone upon the work of Castlereagh at the Congress of Vienna. In appearance what he asked was little, in actuality what he secured was sufficient to seal England's triumph. First and foremost to be noted is the restoration of the balance of power, the maintenance of which, at least against any French disturbance of it, was amply guaranteed by the terms of peace. Not again, indeed, has France seriously disturbed that balance, and, as in the period following the peace of Utrecht, England and France have often found it possible to be friends. More tangible and no less important were the territorial rewards secured by England

in the form of colonies and naval stations. The retention of Ceylon, Cape Colony, and Mauritius gave her
unquestioned control of the sea route to India. Malta
and the protectorate over the Ionian Islands established
her predominance in the middle and eastern Mediterranean. In the West Indies the acquisition of Tobago,
St. Lucia, Trinidad, and part of Dutch Guiana merely
increased British predominance in that area.

Looking beyond the peace settlement of Vienna and
its immediate results one may perceive the wider significance of the Second Hundred Years' War. From a
power with little influence upon continental affairs
Britain had become the chief guarantor of the continental balance of power. From a position of merely
one of the naval, commercial, and colonial powers of the
time she had risen to a place of predominance which
has endured to the present day. Thus England was
able to enjoy for a century what she fought more than a
century to obtain. And not only so, for the peaceful
enjoyment of this position for so great a length of time
has made possible the development of that Second British Empire, one of the greatest achievements of the
modern age, one which, whatever may be the position
of England in the future, renders secure her place
among the great powers of history.

BIBLIOGRAPHICAL NOTE

Nothing more is attempted in this bibliography than to list some of the indispensable older works, and to catalogue the more recent important books and periodical articles. Special attention is here paid to books and articles which treat of policy, and the interrelation of policy and strategy, for that is the viewpoint from which the writer has approached the subject in the text. Lists of the older standard works may be found in the bibliographies appended to volumes V, VI, VIII, and IX of the *Cambridge Modern History*. Similar, but briefer, bibliographies will be found in the *Cambridge History of the British Empire*, which is now in process of publication, and in the *Cambridge History of British Foreign Policy*. Other useful bibliographical helps are Channing, Hart, and Turner, *Guide to the Study of American History* (Boston, 1912); R. G. Trotter, *Canadian History: a Syllabus and Guide to Reading* (New York, 1926); and the bibliographical chapter in R. G. Thwaites, *France in America* (volume VII of the American Nation Series). Many special works contain extensive bibliographies which the student may consult for references to special phases of the subject.

As a general approach to the subject the student might well read Admiral A. T. Mahan's classic work, *The Influence of Sea Power upon History, 1660-1783* (Boston, 1890). Mahan's conclusions concerning the influence of sea power upon British policy and strategy, and upon the outcome of the Anglo-French wars, have never been seriously challenged. R. G. Albion, in his *Forests and Sea Power* (Harvard University Press, 1926), discusses the problem of naval stores and its importance in relation to the policy of the chief naval powers. For a study of British foreign policy the *Cambridge History of British Foreign Policy*, edited by Sir A. W. Ward and G. P. Gooch (3 vols., New

York, 1922-1923), is indispensable. Volume I contains an introductory section on British policy to 1783 and a more detailed account of the same in the period 1783-1815. H. E. Egerton, *British Foreign Policy in Europe* (London, 1917), is a helpful and suggestive work.

The beginnings of Anglo-French commercial rivalry are described by D. G. E. Hall, "Anglo-French Trade Relations Under Charles II," in *History* VII (1922), 17-30, and by L. B. Packard, "International Rivalry and Free Trade Origins, 1660-1678," in the *Quarterly Journal of Economics* XXXVIII (1923), 412-435. For Anglo-French colonial rivalry the student should consult the *Cambridge History of the British Empire*, edited by J. H. Rose, A. P. Newton, and E. A. Benians (Cambridge University Press, 1929-). The chapters in H. L. Osgood, *The American Colonies in the Eighteenth Century* (4 vols., Columbia University Press, 1924-1925), which treat of Anglo-French colonial relations, will be found suggestive and helpful. The works of Francis Parkman are still standard for the Canadian phases of Anglo-French rivalry. His *Count Frontenac and New France Under Louis XIV, Half Century of Conflict*, and *Montcalm and Wolfe,* cover the period 1688-1763. A recent useful summary of the same subject is G. M. Wrong, *The Rise and Fall of New France* (2 vols., New York, 1928). The best account of Anglo-French fur trade rivalry is that of C. H. McIlwain in his Introduction to *Wraxall's Abridgment of the New York Indian Records* (Harvard University Press, 1915). Other phases of the same subject are developed by W. T. Morgan, "English Fear of 'Encirclement' in the Seventeenth Century," in the *Canadian Historical Review* X (1929), 4-22, and by A. H. Buffinton, "The Policy of Albany and English Westward Expansion," in the *Mississippi Valley Historical Review* VIII (1922), 327-366. Early phases of Anglo-French rivalry in New England are treated by Viola F. Barnes in *The Dominion of New England* (Yale University Press, 1923). Anglo-French and Anglo-Spanish rivalry in the South is best described by Verner W. Crane in *The Southern Frontier, 1670-1732* (Duke University

Press, 1928). For Anglo-French rivalry in the West Indies S. L. Mims, *Colbert's West India Policy* (Yale University Press, 1912), C. S. S. Higham, *The Development of the Leeward Islands Under the Restoration, 1660-1688* (Cambridge University Press, 1921), and F. W. Pitman, *The Development of the British West Indies, 1700-1763* (Yale University Press, 1917), may be consulted.

The economic aspects of the early Anglo-French wars are described by G. N. Clark in *The Dutch Alliance and the War Against French Trade* (Manchester University Press, 1923), and in an article in the *Economic History Review* I (1928), 262-280, entitled "War Trade and Trade War, 1701-1713." J. S. Corbett, *England in the Mediterranean* (2 vols., London, 1904), describes the beginnings of English policy and strategy in that area. For the war in the colonies and British colonial policy at this time the student may consult G. H. Guttridge, *The Colonial Policy of William III in America and the West Indies* (Cambridge University Press, 1922) and these articles by W. T. Morgan: "The Origins of the South Sea Company," in the *Political Science Quarterly* XLIV (1929), 16-38; "The South Sea Company and the Canadian Expedition in the Reign of Queen Anne," in the *Hispanic American Review* VIII (1928), 143-166; and "Some Attempts at Imperial Cooperation in the Reign of Queen Anne," in the *Transactions of the Royal Historical Society*, 4th Series, volume X (1927), 171-194.

British policy in the period between the second and third Anglo-French wars is described by Basil Williams in a series of articles in the *English Historical Review*, volumes XV and XVI, entitled "The Foreign Policy of England Under Walpole." The same subject is treated by Paul Vaucher in his *Robert Walpole et la Politique de Fleury, 1731-1742* (Paris, 1924). The best study of Anglo-French commercial rivalry in this period is that of C. M. Andrews, "Anglo-French Commercial Rivalry, 1700-1750: the Western Phase," in the *American Historical Review* XX (1914-1915), 539-556 and 761-780. Several recent studies have thrown light upon Anglo-Spanish commercial and colonial rivalry leading to the war of 1739. To be noted are H. W. V. Temperley, "The Causes of the War of Jenkins' Ear," in the *Transactions of the Royal Historical Society,* 3d Series, volume III (1909), 197-236; Vera L. Brown, "The South Sea Company and Contraband Trade," in the *American Historical Review* XXXI (1925-1926), 662-678, and "Contraband Trade: a Factor in the Decline of Spain's Empire in America," in the *Hispanic American Review* VIII (1928), 178-189; A. S. Aiton, "The Asiento Treaty as Reflected in the Papers of Lord Shelburne," in the same journal, volume VIII, 167-177.

A recent volume dealing with the naval aspects of the third Anglo-French war is H. W. Richmond, *The Navy in the War of 1739-1748* (Cambridge University Press, 1920). J. S. McLennan, *Louisbourg from its Foundation to its Fall, 1713-1758* (London, 1918), is authoritative for the history of that fortress and its capture in 1745. A valuable recent study of certain phases of British policy during this war is Sir Richard Lodge, "The Hanau Controversy of 1744 and the Fall of Carteret," in the *English Historical Review* XXXVIII (1923), 509-531.

In the period between the third and fourth wars Anglo-French rivalry in America centered in Acadia and the Ohio valley. A very satisfactory treatment of English policy in Acadia is that of J. B. Brebner, *New England's Outpost: Acadia before the Conquest of Canada* (Columbia University Press, 1927). A valuable study of the English advance into the Ohio valley is A. T. Volwiler, *George Croghan and the Westward Movement, 1741-1782* (Cleveland, 1926).

The most useful brief accounts of the Anglo-French contest for India are Sir A. C. Lyall, *The Rise and Expansion of the British Dominion in India* (5th ed., London, 1910), and P. E. Roberts, *The History of India to the End of the East India Company* (Oxford, 1916). The forthcoming volume IV of the *Cambridge History of the British Empire,* entitled *British India, 1497-1858,* will doubtless be indispensable. Valuable recent studies of Anglo-French rivalry in the period of the third and fourth wars are Sir George

Forrest, *The Life of Lord Clive* (2 vols., London, 1918);
Henry Dodwell, *Dupleix and Clive* (London, 1920); and
Alfred Martineau, *Dupleix et l'Inde Française* (3 vols.,
Paris, 1920-1927).

The standard work on the Seven Years' War is R. P.
Waddington, *La Guerre de Sept Ans* (5 vols., Paris, 1899-
1914). The same writer has a study of the Diplomatic
Revolution, *Louis XV et le Renversement des Alliances,
1754-1756* (Paris, 1896). The best general study of British
policy and strategy in this war is J. S. Corbett, *England in
the Seven Years' War* (2 vols., London, 1907). English
policy may also be studied in the two recent lives of Pitt,
Basil Williams, *The Life of William Pitt, Earl of Chatham*
(2 vols., New York, 1913), and Albert von Ruville, *William
Pitt, Earl of Chatham* (English translation, 3 vols., New
York, 1907). The title of Kate Hotblack's work, *Chatham's Colonial Policy: a Study in the Fiscal and Economic
Implications of the Colonial Policy of the Elder Pitt* (New
York, 1917), is sufficiently indicative of its character; it is a
valuable study. The same writer has defended Pitt's views
of the peace in an article on "The Peace of Paris, 1763," in
the *Transactions of the Royal Historical Society*, 3d Series,
volume II (1908), 235-267. Another useful biographical
study, revealing the political cross currents of the time, is
Henry Fox, First Lord Holland (2 vols., Oxford, 1911) by
Thad W. Riker. England's relations with Prussia are described by Sir Richard Lodge, *Great Britain and Prussia in
the Eighteenth Century* (Oxford, 1923), and by J. H. Rose
in two articles in volume XXIX of the *English Historical
Review*, entitled "Frederick the Great and England, 1756-
1763." A valuable study of British opinion in relation to
questions of commerce and colonial policy in the period
1754-1783 is G. B. Hertz, *The Old Colonial System* (Manchester University Press, 1905).

For some of the later phases of Anglo-Bourbon colonial
rivalry, including the Falkland Islands crisis of 1770, the
student may consult the exhaustive study of Vera L. Brown,
"Anglo-Spanish Relations in America in the Closing Years

of the Colonial Era, 1763-1774," in the *Hispanic American Review* V (1922), 325-483.

The best brief study of French policy in relation to the American Revolution is E. S. Corwin, *French Policy and the American Alliance of 1778* (Princeton University Press, 1916). The same writer has stated his conclusions more briefly in an article in volume XXI of the *American Historical Review*. In the same volume C. H. Van Tyne has stated somewhat different conclusions in an article entitled, "The Influences Which Determined the French Government to Make the Treaty with America, 1778." Professor Van Tyne has also discussed the subject of "French Aid Before the Alliance of 1778," in volume XXXI of the same periodical. Another recent study of French policy is Alfred Dumaine, "Le Comte de Vergennes et l'Indépendence des Etats-Unis," in volume XXXVIII of the *Revue d'Histoire Diplomatique*. A well-documented study of Spanish policy is Dr. Juan F. Yela Utrilla, *España ante la Independencia de los Estados Unidos* (2 vols., 2d edition, Lérida, 1925). The diplomatic contest for the West is adequately described by P. C. Phillips, *The West in the Diplomacy of the American Revolution* (University of Illinois Studies in the Social Sciences, volume II, Urbana, 1913).

The British conduct of the war is discussed by W. M. James in *The British Navy in Adversity* (London, 1926), and by G. H. Guttridge in an article on "Lord George Germain in Office, 1775-1782," in the *American Historical Review* XXXIII (1927-1928), 23-43. The decisive Yorktown campaign is well described by Rear Admiral F. E. Chadwick in a paper in the *Report of the American Historical Association* for 1915, entitled "Sea Power: the Decisive Factor in Our Struggle for Independence." A well-documented account of *The Armed Neutralities of 1780 and 1800* has been published by the Carnegie Endowment for International Peace, edited by James Brown Scott (New York, 1918).

The rapprochement of England and France after the peace of 1783 is described by J. H. Rose, "The Franco-

British Commercial Treaty of 1786," in the *English Historical Review* XXIII (1908), 709-724. The cause of the outbreak of war between England and France in 1793 is a debatable question. For an elaboration of the view expressed in the text the reader is referred to J. H. Rose, *William Pitt and the Great War* (London, 1914), which is also the best study of Pitt's war policy. Oscar Browning, in his "England and France in 1793," in the *Fortnightly Review* for February, 1883, has argued that war might have been avoided. W. T. Laprade, *England and the French Revolution* (Johns Hopkins University Studies in Historical and Political Science, volume XXVII, Baltimore, 1909), argues that Pitt precipitated war to ruin a commercial rival. Another useful work on British policy is E. D. Adams, *The Influence of Grenville on Pitt's Foreign Policy, 1787-1798* (The Carnegie Institution of Washington, 1904).

The best account of the naval, commercial, and colonial phases of the wars of 1793-1815 is Admiral A. T. Mahan's *The Influence of Sea Power upon the French Revolution and Empire* (2 vols., Boston, 1898). The same phases of these wars are emphasized by J. H. Rose in a volume of essays entitled *The Indecisiveness of Modern War and Other Essays* (London, 1927). The same writer has described "The Political Reactions of Bonaparte's Eastern Expedition," in the *English Historical Review* XLIV (1929), 48-58. J. F. Rippy's *Latin America in World Politics* (New York, 1929) is a useful summary of the effects of the European conflict upon Latin America. A more detailed study of certain phases of the same subject is W. S. Robertson's *Francisco de Miranda and the Revolutionizing of Spanish America*, printed in volume I of the *Report of the American Historical Association* for 1907. Certain aspects of Anglo-French commercial rivalry in the Near and Middle East in this period are well summarized in H. L. Hoskins, *British Routes to India* (New York, 1928). Waldemar Ekedahl discusses "The Principal Causes of the Renewal of War Between England and France in 1803" in the *Transactions of the Royal Historical Society*, New

Series, volume VIII (1894), 181-201. In volume XIX of
the *American Historical Review* Professor W. E. Lingelbach
published a valuable article on "Historical Investigation
and the Commercial History of the Napoleonic Era," sum-
marizing results to that date (1914). The student may still
read with profit the article of J. H. Rose on "Napoleon and
English Commerce" in the *English Historical Review* VIII
(1893), 704-725. The most valuable recent study of the
Continental System is F. E. Melvin, *Napoleon's Navigation
System: a Study of Trade Control During the Continental
Blockade* (University of Pennsylvania Press, 1919). Another recent study of the same subject, which has not been
wholly acceptable to experts, but which contains useful
material, is E. F. Heckscher, *The Continental System: an
Economic Interpretation* (Oxford, 1922). Finally, it may
be noted that the relation of Anglo-French rivalry to the
ultimate liberation of the Spanish American colonies is
authoritatively discussed by Dexter Perkins in *The Monroe
Doctrine, 1823-1826* (Harvard University Press, 1927).

INDEX